MILEY
CYRUS
A-Z

MILEY
CYRUS

SARAH OLIVER

JOHN BLAKE

Published by John Blake Publishing Ltd,
3 Bramber Court, 2 Bramber Road,
London W14 9PB, England

www.johnblakepublishing.co.uk

First published in paperback in 2011

ISBN: 978-1-84358-299-1

British Library Cataloguing-in-Publication Data:

A catalogue record for this book is available from the British Library.

Design by www.envydesign.co.uk

Printed in Great Britain by CPI Bookmarque, Croydon, CR0 4TD

1 3 5 7 9 10 8 6 4 2

Papers used by John Blake Publishing are natural, recyclable products made
from wood grown in sustainable forests. The manufacturing processes
conform to the environmental regulations of the country of origin.

Every attempt has been made to contact the relevant copyright-holders,
but some were unobtainable. We would be grateful if the appropriate
people could contact us.

Dedicated with love to my sister Liz,
the best sister in the world.

Other A–Z books by Sarah Oliver

Justin Bieber A–Z
One Direction A-Z
The Wanted A–Z
Taylor Lautner A–Z
Robert Pattinson A–Z
The Completely Unofficial *Glee* A–Z

INTRODUCTION

The *Miley Cyrus A–Z* is jam-packed with everything you need to know about Miley. No other book goes into so much detail or tells all the set secrets about Hannah Montana and her movies. Read all about her kissing scenes and the crazy things she gets up to when the cameras aren't rolling.

Sarah Oliver is a celebrity journalist who knows more about Miley than any other writer on the planet. She has worked with Miley fans across the world to produce the most up-to-date guide to everyone's favourite teen actress and singer.

You can read this book from start to finish, or dip in and out of it, as you prefer.

A is for...

Accidents

Miley might be a hugely successful actress and singer but that doesn't mean things always go right for her. She has had her fair share of accidents, but thankfully she's never seriously hurt herself.

When she was filming *Hannah Montana: The Movie* Miley had two accidents on the same day. She told *TOTP* magazine what happened: 'I busted my face. I tripped over a wire that was in the grass and totally busted it. I was having the worst day because when I went in my trailer, I fractured my ankle falling up the stairs. My mom was like, "I don't know how anybody falls up the stairs and breaks their ankle".'

Normally when someone breaks their ankle they are ordered to stay in bed and rest but Miley couldn't. She didn't want to let people down and insisted that they continued to film the movie. Her ankle was placed in a cast and even though she couldn't do everything she usually did, she carried on and did her best. When you watch the movie you can't even tell that she's injured.

Miley seems to be very accident prone and even managed to hurt herself while eating a piece of chicken. She posted a video on YouTube to explain to her fans what had happened but had to have her friend Mandy translate because it had damaged her throat and she couldn't speak properly.

Miley said, 'The reason I sound like this is because I cut my uvula. The way the nurse explained it to me is, you know that cartoon when that really obnoxious baby screams and you see that waggling thing around in their mouth? That's an uvula. So I cut my uvula today on a piece of chicken. I put too much dressing on it, it was too slippery and it got caught and it cut my uvula.'

Ouch! That must have been so painful. Thankfully she didn't do herself any lasting damage and was back singing shortly afterwards.

Poor Miley had another accident when she decided she wanted to go out without anyone recognising her. She got herself a wig but thought it wasn't quite right, so she decided to straighten it. She was happily straightening each section until she smelt smoke and realised that the wig was on fire!

When we have accidents there might only be ourselves or a few friends to witness what has happened, but for Miley sometimes there are thousands of fans watching her when things go wrong. When she was on stage performing 'I Got Nerve' at one of her The Best of Both Worlds concerts her dancers threw her up in the air. However, instead of catching her they accidentally dropped Miley and she landed on the floor. Miley didn't let it put her off and jumped up eager to carry on performing. That must have taken real guts because the natural thing would have been for her to burst into tears and insist on having some time out.

Another time Miley might have felt like crying was when she was on the red carpet at a big awards show and a bee decided to sting her. She couldn't cry because there were lots of camera crews from all around the world there and they would have filmed her. She had to keep smiling while trying to get inside the venue as quickly as she possibly could.

Miley's also run into glass doors thinking there was nothing there, and fallen off a chair when getting ready for a radio interview. Thankfully none of these accidents were recorded – so she doesn't have to suffer the embarrassment of seeing them on YouTube.

Acting

Acting has been one of Miley's passions for a very long time. She started out doing music videos and little things with her dad when his singing career was at its peak. She was only six but really enjoyed working alongside him. It was about two years later when she decided that she wanted to be an actress. Her parents didn't pressurise her but Miley knew being an actress would make her happy.

Her dad Billy Ray was a very popular country singer in the 1990s, and he had millions of fans. He is best known for his number one single 'Achy Breaky Heart' which came out a few months before Miley was born. He explained to the *San Francisco Chronicle* how he found out she wanted to act: 'We saw the play *Mamma Mia*, and halfway through it Miley nudged me and said, "This is what I want to do. I want to be a great actress."'

DID YOU KNOW?

Miley actually sang a song from *Mamma Mia* in one of her *Hannah Montana* auditions.

Miley got her first proper acting job when she was living in Toronto. She had spent lots of time on the set of her dad's show *Doc*, so was thrilled when she was asked in 2001 if she'd like to be in an episode. She played a character called Kiley who had just moved with her dad into the same apartment block as Doc (played by Miley's dad). If Miley loved acting before, she loved acting a million times more after playing Kiley.

It wasn't a surprise to her family when Miley was asked to be in *Doc* because every week she would pester her dad and ask him if he'd got a new script and if she'd been written in. Every week was disappointing until she got asked to play Kiley.

Up until that point Miley hadn't had any formal training so she set about going to as many acting classes and camps as she could. She wanted to be the best actress she could and needed to learn as much as possible to be able to compete against much more experienced child actors at auditions. She wasn't interested in building snowmen or going sledging – she just wanted to be in a theatre practising every minute she could.

Since her appearance on *Doc*, Miley hasn't stopped learning how to act. Peter Chelsom directed Miley in *Hannah Montana: The Movie* and he wanted to teach her how to improve her focus and concentration in scenes.

He explained to online entertainment news agency BANG Showbiz what they did: 'We did stuff before we started filming that was just the kind of stuff you'd do at drama school, you know. Did I give her a detention? No. I made her read a sonnet though. A Shakespeare sonnet. She said, "Oh no, I can't." I said, "Let's do it because it'll be the most difficult thing you'll ever do." We did all that kind of stuff. It was remarkable.

'We used to have this code where I would say, "This means focus, because I don't want to have to shout at you across the set!"'

When Miley first started acting she tried to lose her accent because there weren't many parts that required girls to have southern accents. When she was cast as Hannah she went with her new and improved accent but the people in charge didn't like it. They wanted the real Miley and her Tennessee accent. Miley quickly went back to using her real accent and that is the voice she uses in her TV shows and movies.

Miley loves acting so much that she can't decide whether she likes acting or singing the most. She loves playing a character and being on a movie set when acting but enjoys expressing herself through music, too. It sounds like she'll always be an actress AND a singer.

Miley might have had huge success with *Hannah Montana* but she doesn't want to play similar types of characters all the time. She wants to stretch herself and take on completely different roles. She wouldn't be scared of doing a movie that would be too old for her *Hannah Montana* fans to watch either. She isn't afraid to think outside the box.

She revealed to the *Telegraph*: 'I'm kind of bipolar in my acting choices because I just want to do a little bit of everything. One day I'm telling my mom, you know, I want to do an action movie and then I want to be doing comedy and then all different types of things. I get a little bored so hopefully I'll get a chance to do a little bit of everything.'

If you'd like to follow in Miley's footsteps and become an actress, she has some advice for you. Miley revealed in a Q&A session with fans in *USA Today*: 'Start taking singing lessons, acting lessons, dance lessons. When you're younger, get training, so when you are a little bit older and you can start going on auditions, you do have one-up on everyone. You should definitely go for it, but take your time and train.'

Animals

Miley is animal mad! She has always been brought up around lots of animals so cares a great deal about the way they are treated.

She told *Office Max* during a Q&A session with fans: 'I have lots of horses, kitty cats, dogs, chickens and fish. My dogs are on tour with me. We love animals. My dad had a pet squirrel for a while that kept coming around. He loves animals, too [laughs]. He makes eggs and bacon every morning for my dogs.'

In 2009 Miley re-homed some chickens that were used on the set of *Hannah Montana: The Movie* because she wanted to give them a better life on her Tennessee farm. She sneaked on set and whisked them away before anyone could stop her. Animal charity PETA were so impressed that they gave her a Compassionate Citizen Award. PETA Assistant Director Dan Shannon told the press: 'Miley's heart is as big as her smile…We hope that her act of compassion will inspire her fans to be kind to animals too.'

Miley has always loved watching the chickens on the Cyrus farm so she'll no doubt enjoying seeing her new additions enjoying their new life every time she goes back to Tennessee. The farm is quite isolated so when Miley was growing up she couldn't nip next door to play with other kids. Instead she had to play with her brothers and sisters… and their animals.

Even though she's a megastar and living in Los Angeles most of the time she still walks her dogs like a normal teenager. She doesn't need someone to do it for her and it's clear from the smile on her face as she walks them that she enjoys spending some one-on-one time with her doggy pals.

When she first moved to LA, Miley and her sister Brandi actually tried to set up their own dog-walking service but it didn't work out. No one would hire them. They put up signs everywhere but they didn't get a single phone call. In five years' time Miley says she would like to be a professional dog walker if she's not still acting and singing. There's not much chance of this happening, though, because she's likely to be an even bigger star by then. She'll be too busy releasing hit records.

The Cyrus family has so many dogs. They have a German Shepherd called Texas T (or Tex) – he's Billy Ray's favourite and travels with him everywhere. They also own a Shih Tzu called Loco who lives with the family in LA; Miley's little sister Noah loves this dog the most. Another German Shepherd called Rosie lives in Nashville. Fluke is a Labrador and Beagle cross who spends some of his time in LA and some of it in Nashville;

they also have a black Shih Tzu called Juicy. Miley bought Yorkshire Terrier Rodeo (or Roadie) after visiting the Houston Rodeo Show in March 2006. The year after she acquired another Yorkshire Terrier called Shooter. When Miley turned sixteen she was given a Maltese Poodle cross puppy who she called Sofie after her grandad's dog. Not long after, she got Mate, a white German Shepherd – naming him Mate because that's what she called Liam Hemsworth (who she was dating at the time), after one of his favourite words.

As well as dogs Miley has a white rabbit called Jack who lives in LA, seven horses who live in Nashville (Memphis is her favourite), three cats who also live in Nashville, twelve birds, a donkey and a gecko. She did have a goat called Billy but he died.

Auditioning

Miley's first audition happened by accident. It was a TV advert for Banquet Foods and she only went along to watch some kids she knew audition. They were too young for the part but Miley wasn't and the kids' mum suggested that Miley try. Miley did really well and got the part. Unfortunately, because it was so long ago the advert is no longer showing and isn't available online either so fans can't see Miley in action.

For *Hannah Montana*, however, the audition process was a lot more complicated and Miley had to keep fighting to make it to the next round. At first she was told that she should go for the part of Lilly but deep down she knew she wanted to play Chloe Stewart. Later, when she got the part, they changed the character's name to Miley Stewart to make it less confusing – otherwise Miley would have been acting as Chloe, who is also Hannah!

Miley's agent got Miley to do a tape of her reading Lilly's lines first of all, and sent it to Disney. They must have liked what they saw because they got back to the agent and asked for Miley to do another tape audition – this time reading Chloe Stewart's lines.

Miley told Zap2it: 'I did taping. I did two tapes, four tapes. I started out as Lilly and they wanted me to audition for Hannah Montana and that sounded very positive. They said, "You are too small, too young. Bye-bye." Well, that's rude. So I made another tape. Dang it! They are going to watch my tape and like it!'

One day, out of the blue, when Miley had almost given up hope, she got a call from the people casting *Hannah Montana* asking her to fly out for a proper audition in Los Angeles. Her dream of playing Chloe wasn't over!

Miley decided to wear make-up and her mum's high

heels to make herself look older. When she arrived she saw there were lots of other girls she would have to beat to get the part. 'The audition process for anything is so scary. You walk into a room with sixty girls. In my case, I have to say, if I was them I don't know why they chose me. You can see their head shots and just know they know a lot more than you do. They don't like you – that is the scariest part!' she explained to Zap2it.

Her audition went well but it was until two weeks later that she got the call to say she was a finalist. They had got it down to a final thirty so Miley was only a tiny bit closer to getting the part. Her final audition a few weeks later was probably the toughest because there was just Miley and two other girls. Miley must have been so happy when she was told she was the girl they wanted to play Chloe. She'd had such a long time to wait. She was eleven when she had her first audition, and she filmed her first episode of *Hannah Montana* when she was thirteen!

The show's creators had, in fact, been blown away by Miley in the audition room, but it had taken a while for them to come to the decision to hire Miley because she was so young and inexperienced. The other two girls shortlisted for the part had much more experience. One of the girls was sixteen, so three full years older than Miley, and the other one was Taylor Momsen who'd been in the movie *Spy Kids 2*. When they were weighing up which girl would be best for the job they realised Miley's dad was Billy Ray Cyrus. Before she got down to the final three no one from Disney knew who her dad was because Billy Ray believed it important that Miley get the job because of her own talents, not because she was his daughter.

The creators realised that Miley might have star quality in her genes. They took a chance on her because they wanted to see the magic they'd seen in the audition rooms on TV. They also managed to convince Disney bosses that she was the perfect choice. Miley told Jonathan Ross on his talk show, 'Five minutes before my audition, I spilt Dr Pepper on me and a bird pooped on my head, and apparently that's good luck because I got the part.'

When Billy Ray knew that things were going to change because Miley was going to be playing Hannah Montana he wrote a song about how he was feeling. It was called 'Ready Set Don't Go'. It was about the moment when a father knows he's got to let his daughter go. In the song Billy talks about Miley having ambitions bigger than her town, and that she's waiting for his blessing before she can go. It says that he uses a smile to cover his broken heart and that he's got to let her spread her wings. It's a powerful song, full of raw emotion.

DID YOU KNOW?

If you want to see Miley's auditions for yourself you should check them out on YouTube. Just search for 'Miley Cyrus *Hannah Montana* audition'. You can see Miley's first audition and later ones with her acting and singing alongside her dad. They're great to watch and show why Miley was picked.

Australia

Miley has been to so many countries promoting *Hannah Montana*, her movies and her music, but when she visited Australia in January 2010 it was for purely personal reasons. She had been dating her boyfriend Liam Hemsworth for quite a while and he wanted to show her where he grew up. She was probably quite nervous getting on the plane to go because she would be meeting Liam's family and friends for the first time.

Liam's parents really liked Miley and enjoyed spending time to get to know her. Liam told Michael Yo on the American entertainment show *Daily 10*: 'Yeah, they loved her. It was really cool to show Miley where I'm from and how I grew up, and it's a completely different world to where she's from. We don't have shopping

MILEY AND LIAM
HEMSWORTH

centres or traffic lights or anything like that, where I live, at least.'

Miley really enjoyed exploring Australia and in particular Phillip Island where Liam grew up. She thought it was very similar to Nashville. She also liked not having the paparazzi follow her every move. She was able to be just a normal teenager having fun.

Awards

You don't get to have as much acting talent as Miley and not win awards. She won her first award in 2007 when she was fourteen. It was a huge achievement to win a Nickelodeon Kids' Choice Award and only five months later she picked up a Teen Choice Award.

She has continued to pick up award after award each year. She'll have to get a few trophy cabinets to in which to display them as it won't be long before she's got twenty awards. At the moment the majority of Miley's awards and nominations have been for her acting skills, but soon she'll be picking up more awards and nominations for her music. She definitely has a bright future ahead of her.

OPPOSITE: MILEY ATTENDING THE 2010 AMERICAN MUSIC AWARDS

B is for...

Beauty

In the May 2010 edition of *People* magazine Miley was named one of the World's Most Beautiful People. In 2009 she was voted the Best Dressed by *Teen Vogue*. Some stars might get big heads if major magazines called them beautiful or said they were top dressers, but not Miley. She doesn't feel more beautiful than anyone else and is happy to tell her fans that she still has body hang-ups. She's just a normal girl.

Best Friends

People might envy Miley for being a big star but there are negative sides to being famous. One of them is that it's hard to make friends. You have lots of people trying to be your friend because you're famous, eager to build their own celebrity profile and desperate to sell stories about you to the papers. This means that people like Miley have to watch who they let get close. Thankfully, Miley is a good judge of character.

The *Daily Telegraph* asked Miley what sort of qualities a best friend should have. She said, 'Honesty and trust…It's hard to find people you can trust. I probably only have four or five people who I would fully trust. You know, who would be there for me and tell the truth about me and to me.'

Because Miley is away travelling a lot she can't always see her best friends as often as she'd like. Thankfully she's super close to her mum and sisters so can always talk to them.

Bible

If Miley was shipwrecked on a desert island and could take three things with her one of them would probably be her Bible. She loves reading her Bible and sometimes she stays up late at night reading it. Miley

MILEY WITH EMILY OSMENT

and her family believe that the Bible is different from any other book in the world because you can read it a hundred times and you'd still learn something new each time. She explained to *TV Guide*: 'It's my "how-to" guide for life'.

Miley's Bible has helped her through some tough times. She likes reading the book of Psalms which are songs and poems of praise to God. She says that reading the book of Psalms helped her cope with being bullied, deal with her heart condition and learn that money doesn't matter. She told TV Guide: 'I don't know what I would do without a God that blesses me with the ability to do this'.

Big Fish

After her small part in her dad's TV show *Doc*, and her Banquet Foods' TV advert Miley got a part in a movie in 2003. It was a huge deal for Miley, then aged eleven, and her whole family were thrilled when she was cast as Ruthie in *Big Fish*.

It wasn't the biggest part in the world but that didn't matter to Miley. She only had one line: 'Edward, don't'. She had to say it to a boy as he made his way to the witch's house. There were loads of big stars in the movie like Ewan McGregor, Helena Bonham

Carter and Danny DeVito… and it was being directed by Tim Burton who had directed *Planet of the Apes* and *Batman Returns*.

Big Fish was filmed in Alabama, over 800 miles away from Toronto where they were living at the time, so Miley had to do quite a bit of travelling. Miley must have thought back then that working on a big movie would be glamorous, but it wasn't. Her scene was set in a swamp at night so there were loads of creepy crawlies and it was very cold. Most kids would have quit and told their mums to take them home but not Miley – she loved it. She might have been working in horrible surroundings but she still wanted to be an actress!

Birthdays

Miley loves her birthdays. For her fifteenth birthday she said all she wanted to do was go back to Nashville and eat her grandma's cake. She's so busy all the time that she just wanted a day to chill out with her family close by. However, she didn't get her wish as her family threw her a surprise party and they all dressed up in silly costumes from the eighties. Her dad wore an awful blond mullet wig and hosted the night. He'd arranged for all of Miley's old friends to be there. It was a big surprise for Miley because he was supposed to be on the other side of the USA so she wasn't expecting to see him on her birthday.

The party wasn't held on her actual birthday because she was on tour on that day. She still got to celebrate as she explained to Office Max: 'The whole crew, and we have like 13 semi trucks travelling with us for the tour, the whole crew came on stage and they gave me a beautiful watch as a present that I'll always remember.'

For her sixteenth Miley had the biggest birthday party ever. Thousands of people descended on Disneyland to help her celebrate including, to Miley's delight, her best friend Lesley, and she raised thousands of pounds for charity.

She told GMA before the big event: 'This is gonna be I think like the craziest sweet sixteenth ever because there's like seven thousand people coming, there's seven thousand cupcakes that go out to everyone. I'm like, I don't want to be the person baking the cupcakes because that's going to take a while!'

There was a parade with Miley dressed like a princess, and whole host of other celebrities and Disney characters joined in too. She performed as well because even though it was her birthday she felt like she should give something back to her fans. It was a great night, one that Miley will never forget.

As well as getting to have her party at Disneyland, Miley got some great presents. Her dad treated her to her own recording studio and her mum bought her a puppy called Sofie.

Miley told *TV Guide*: 'I got a dog today, so I couldn't be happier. A little doggie named Sofie. I started crying my eyes off, I was so dorky but I couldn't help it.'

Because Miley's birthday party at Disney was held a month before her actual birthday her friends decided that on the night of Miley's birthday they would throw her a party. It was the night of the American Music Awards so afterwards Taylor Swift and Ashley Tisdale presented her with a huge cake.

Taylor told *Star* magazine: 'Us girls got together and thought it would be fun to do a little surprise party for Miley; she deserves it.'

It's so great that Miley has famous friends like Taylor and Ashley who she can hang out with at big awards shows. They are really close and love spending time together.

For her seventeenth birthday her parents surprised her with an eighties-themed party in New York. Miley's cake was huge: there were four tiers and a mini rocker band made of icing performing on it. The cast of the musical *Rock of Ages* dropped by and performed for her and her guests. There might have been fewer people there than at her sixteenth the year before, but she still had an amazing time.

Miley was hoping to have a chilled out eighteenth. She told *OK!* magazine: 'I hope I can just have a frickin' break... because I haven't had time, even a week to chill. So I'm probably just going to go to the beach or something. I'll take about ten of my friends with me and hang out with the people I never really get to see. A lot of my friends, they work, and I'm in the business too so I'll make sure we carve out some time so we can relax.'

Miley actually ended up having another big party, this time in LA. It was held at the Trousdale club two days before her actual birthday. Miley had just performed at the American Music Awards but she still wanted to stay up late and celebrate her birthday with her celebrity friends. Demi Moore, Ashton Kutcher, Kelly Osbourne and Mark Salling (Puck from *Glee*) came along and they had an amazing night. Her dad couldn't make it because he was working but her mum Tish was there to oversee everything. DJ Cobra was in charge of the music and all the guests tucked into luxury cakes from the Sweet & Saucy Shop.

It was reported the next day that Miley had been spotted kissing teen actor Avan Jogia at her party, but that she was still officially single.

Bolt

In 2008 Miley provided the voice of Penny in the animated movie *Bolt*. Penny is the main human character so Miley had lots of lines. Penny is a twelve-year-old child actress who acts alongside Bolt the dog in a TV show called *Bolt*. She loves him and he helps her deal with being a star. When Bolt goes missing she is devastated but the studio don't care, simply replacing Bolt with another white dog. Bolt makes new furry friends and manages to make it back to Penny; there's a fire and Bolt saves the day. Penny realises that she doesn't want to be in the show any more and moves to the country with Bolt.

Miley really enjoyed being in *Bolt* and felt that children could learn a lot from watching the movie. She explained to *Teen Hollywood*: 'I love all my dogs and I hope that, after seeing this film, people will want to go home and love their dog. I hope kids realise, one, that you love your pets and know what great friends they can be. And two, that no matter what you do for a living, you have to realise that that can go away in a second.'

Miley recorded *Bolt*'s theme song, 'I Thought I Lost You'. It's a beautiful track and earned her an MTV Award for Best Song from a Movie. It was also nominated for a Golden Globe and a Critics Choice Award too.

MILEY WITH JOHN TRAVOLTA AT THE *BOLT* PREMIERE

Braison

Miley's younger brother is called Braison and he is two years younger than her. He might be her little brother but he's quite a bit taller than her. They have very different personalities, as Miley explained in a tweet in July 2009. She posted two pictures of them standing next to each other and wrote: 'How ironic. My brother is wearing all black and I am wearing all white. Story of our life together. Brothers and sisters are as similar as hands and feet.'

Like most little brothers, Braison enjoys winding Miley up and once when she asked him if he'd be in a band with her he turned her down, saying he was too good for her.

Braison has done a bit of acting himself. Like Miley he was in an episode of *Doc* and he appeared in an episode of *Hannah Montana* back in 2008. But acting isn't his passion and he prefers playing basketball. He likes playing one on one and putting Billy Ray through his paces but missed being able to play basketball with his dad when Billy Ray was one of the contestants on *Dancing with the Stars*. Braison, Miley and the rest of the Cyrus family loved going to the studio to cheer him on but he wasn't the best dancer by a long shot. Still, he managed to finish in fifth place, which was a good achievement.

MILEY AND BRAISON

Like the rest of the Cyrus family, Braison is quite musical and he's in a band called Lazy Randy with his friends Josh Reaves and Lashette Showers. In her parents' home Miley has her own wing, so she has several rooms all to herself where she can just chill out and enjoy being on her own. Her brother Braison is two rooms away, which can be very annoying as she explained to the host of American TV show *The View*: 'He just got a drum set, it's torture. I hate it.' When he's playing it late at night Miley tries to get him to stop by telling him that its 11pm but it doesn't work. He says that if it was Miley playing she wouldn't get into trouble because he thinks she gets to have her music on loud all the time. They definitely have a love/hate relationship.

Brandi

Brandi is Miley's oldest sister. She has the same mum as Miley but a different dad. Billy Ray adopted her when she was really small and has brought her up. Brandi is six years older than Miley and doesn't live at home any more, but she still visits a lot. She is the person Miley tells her deepest secrets to because she knows Brandi won't tell anyone. They are really close and like spending time together on their own. They are often snapped by the paparazzi going to restaurants or going shopping.

Brandi has done a bit of acting alongside Miley and on her own too. She has been in *The Real Miley Cyrus*, *Billy Ray Cyrus: Home at Last*, an episode of *Hannah Montana* and *Zoey 101*. Brandi's real passion is music and she's in a band called Frank and Derol. She is the guitarist and also writes their songs. Brandi, Codi and Megan are looking for a record deal and are performing as much as they can in the meantime. Brandi has lots of confidence on stage because she played the guitar for Miley when she was touring and also on *Hannah Montana*.

If you want to learn more about Brandi and the rest of the Cyrus family you should follow her on Twitter. She is forever updating her fans on what she is doing and what she has planned: twitter.com/theBrandiCyrus

Bret Michaels

Miley was honoured to record a duet with Bret Michaels from the band Poison. Her mum is a huge Poison fan and Miley went to a Poison concert with her when she was younger.

Miley recorded 'Nothin' to Lose' with Bret for his album 'Custom Built'. When some critics heard that

MILEY PERFORMING
WITH BRET MICHAELS

they had recorded 'Nothin' to Lose' they decided to attack Miley and Bret, saying that the lyrics were unsuitable as Miley was a young girl and Bret was so much older. Bret and Miley couldn't believe how much was blown out of proportion. Bret had written the song years before and hadn't intended for it be sung as a duet, and Miley's mum Tish had been in the recording studio with them. There was no scandal! Miley also covered Bret's track 'Every Rose Has Its Thorn' for her album *Can't Be Tamed*.

Britney Spears

Miley might have grown up listening to great country music stars but the first CD she ever bought was Britney Spears' *Hit Me Baby One More Time*. This album made Miley realise how good pop music could be and she wanted to hear more.

Because she took part in competitive cheerleading Miley had to perform to Britney's and other popular pop tracks. She must have learnt them off by heart as she had to make sure she came in at the right time and did her flips at the same time as the other girls. It was important that they all came in on time to secure the highest marks.

She did cover 'I Love Rock and Roll' on *Hannah*

Montana and wouldn't rule out covering more Britney tracks in the future. She particularly likes making tracks that have been forgotten popular again.

In many ways Miley wants to be like Britney when she's touring because she always wants to give her audience something new and exciting. She believes that Britney and Michael Jackson really inspired her when she was growing up so she loves mentioning them on her track 'Party in the USA'.

Now Miley doesn't bother buying pop albums; she just picks the odd pop track for her iPod instead. She is a huge Lady Gaga fan and really loves her songs. If she's at a party she thinks 'Bad Romance' is the best song to put on to get the party started. She loves it so much that she knows all the dance moves.

Her favourite band is Nevada, which many people think is a strange choice because their songs are nothing like Miley's, but she thinks they're great.

Bullying

It might seem that Miley has it all, but she has been plagued by bullies virtually all of her life. When she was at school even her own friends turned against her and did everything they could to make Miley miserable every single day. They locked her in the bathroom and did some awful things that Miley doesn't like to talk about in case it scares her fans. For ages Miley kept what was happening to her a secret but one day her dad overheard her on the phone and went to the principal. They realised then that the bullies had been bullying Miley for a long time and wanted to involve the police. This really scared Miley; she didn't want the police to be involved and wanted to leave. Now she tells her fans in a similar position that they need to tell someone what's happening before it gets to the stage it did with her. She wants them to not be afraid of being afraid.

Miley revealed what it was like on *The View* talk show: 'They were the bigger girls, they were like, "We'll keep you safe if you're not friends with Miley" [to the other girls in Miley's class]. I remember this one day, it was lunch time and we had assigned seats because things were getting that out of control that people weren't even allowed to sit near each other and there was assigned seat day, but wherever you sat that was were you were for the rest of the year… and no one sat by me, so for the rest of the year I sat alone every day. That's the scariest part, just being alone.'

Back then Miley didn't really understand why they hated her so much, but now she thinks it was because her dad was famous and they had money. She loved performing but she was always forced to be at the back in school productions and the bullies always got the lead parts. That must have made Miley feel even worse and she must have wondered why she was being punished.

She talked about what they did to knock her confidence to Tyra Banks: 'I remember when I was in school they had this picture of me that was seriously the worst picture of me you've ever seen. I was always really little and I remember going to the gym one day and we all had to get weighed, which first of all I just don't like that anyway because I don't think you should have to get weighed in front of your peers, and it just makes girls uncomfortable.'

She continued, 'And I was always smaller than everyone else and I remember them being like "Ah, she's so small"… I think that's when it was really like, "We can get her" type thing. And there was this picture of me where I was just so little. I was standing next to them and you could really see the contrast. They had it on their binder every day and they were like showing me the picture of us standing beside each other trying to scare me, and when you really look at it its scary. Scary thoughts.'

Miley must have been so happy when she left and started being home-schooled instead. She really felt that God had rescued her from an impossible situation. Those bullies must be so jealous of Miley now.

Years might have passed since then but Miley is still being bullied on a regular basis by bloggers and people on online forums who write insults about the way she looks. One day Miley decided that enough was enough and hit back at bloggers who had written that she had 'jiggling thighs'.

Miley tweeted: 'Talk all you want. I have my flaws. I'm a normal girl, there's things about my body I would change but stop with calling me f*t in post. I don't even like the word. Those remarks that you hateful people use are fighting words. The ones that scar people and cause them to do damage to themselves or others.

'People that are so okay with being so hateful disgust me and need to spend less time on a gossip website and more time a. reading your Bible, b. reading stories/articles about what happens when cyber abuse and name calling happens. Kids hurt themselves. This is not something to be taken lightly. I know these "message boards" are "no big deal" to YOU but it is to the victim. This has got to stop!!!

'Oh and P.S. if your thighs don't jiggle go see a doctor. Thanks.'

Miley ended her tweet with a link to a cyber-bullying website so that her fans could get more information if they wanted advice. In the future it would be great if Miley could front an anti-bullying campaign. She is a great role model to young girls everywhere because she is proof that you shouldn't let bullies pull you down. If she had listened to the girls at school when they told her she was pathetic and a waste of space she wouldn't be the star she is now.

C is for...

Cameos

Miley is so popular that most directors would give anything to have her in their movie. They know that if she's in their movie then a lot of her fans will go and see it. When a star plays him or herself in a movie and only appears briefly it is called a cameo. Miley had a cameo in *Sex And The City 2*.

Miley might not have had a big part but she was so excited to be involved and have the opportunity to meet Sarah Jessica Parker, Kim Cattrall, Kristin Davis and Cynthia Nixon.

They were equally as excited to meet Miley. Sarah

MILEY ON THE SET OF *SEX AND THE CITY 2*

Jessica Parker told MTV: 'Did you know that she's tall? She's like a Viking. I had no idea! She's a beautiful young lady and very self-possessed. I literally was not in the scene with her. I was in the scene, but we were not [on screen] together. But she was lovely and on time and professional, very sweet. She worked two hours and she was in and out.'

Miley told Ryan Seacrest on his 102.7 KIIS FM radio show: 'It was literally like the best job I've ever done, and it was like a total dream come true. It was so cool…working with Kim [Cattrall] was really cool and Sarah Jessica Parker was like the nicest person in the world.'

It sounds like Miley would be keen to star in *Sex And The City 3* should another movie be made.

Can't Be Tamed

Can't Be Tamed is Miley's third studio album and was first released in Germany, Australia and Poland on 18 June 2010, before being released in the UK and USA on 21 June. She was involved in writing all the tracks but was helped by some great songwriters who helped her make the tracks the best they could be.

She gushed on American talk show *Live With Regis and Kelly*: 'I work with really good people, you know, that I'm able to collaborate with and so it's…someone to look at and look up to and they have good opinions but they also, you know, are totally okay when I say, "No, I know that this is the way I want it to sound." Because at the end of the day it's got my name on it.'

Every album that Miley produces she wants to make better than the one before. She wants to make great music that her fans will love and blast out of their stereos.

Miley wrote the title track 'Can't Be Tamed' with two of her closest friends and she liked the way the song reflects how she feels – she can't be tamed. She doesn't like it when people try and put her in a box and define her. She isn't just a Disney kid any more; she's grown up and she's changed into a woman with her own ideas and her own aspirations. The message behind the song is that you should follow your heart, and produce the kind of music you want rather than what other people say you should. Miley wants her fans to not be afraid of being creative and expressing themselves. She wants to help them deal with the pressures they might be feeling as they try to live up to their parents' expectations.

The video for 'Can't Be Tamed' showed a sexier side to Miley, but that's because she's no longer a little girl. She loved the idea of playing a bird that's stuck in captivity and wearing gorgeous costumes. The silver corset she wore cost an incredible $25,000 and was made out of metal and feathers. Miley is glad she didn't have to pay for it but she didn't get to keep it – once the director shouted cut she had to give it back. She's spent so many years trying on many different outfits for photo shoots and when playing Hannah that she's finally figured out what she likes to wear to be herself.

Shooting the video was a bit daunting for Miley because Liam Hemsworth brought his mum and dad along to watch. They hadn't seen Miley the singer before; they'd only seen her on the beach in Australia chilling out, so it must have been strange for them seeing her with giant wings acting scary. They were seeing Miley the superstar for the first time.

Miley says she never wants to disrespect *Hannah Montana* because it has made her who she is today, but in many ways she's been like a bird in a cage with clipped wings. She's had to try and forget any ideas of her own because they didn't suit the girly image of Hannah. Now she's older she's trying to drop some of the restraints and do the things she has always wanted to. She wants to be free.

Miley's track 'Robot' echoes this. It's about people telling someone what their image should and shouldn't be, and that person making the decision to have the image they want instead. Miley wants people to show their independence and not care what others think. She thinks that a lot of songs are about 'nothing', just going out and finding guys. Miley wants to show that there's more to life than that. She isn't against these types of songs; she just wants to write songs that are deeper.

Miley loved performing her *Hannah Montana* tracks but nothing compared to singing her tracks from *Can't Be Tamed* because she was involved in writing them herself. Every song means something to her, and triggers real emotions when she is performing.

Charity

Miley is one of the kindest people you could ever meet. She might earn millions every year but she gives a lot to charity and helps out at charity events. She knows from reading her Bible that she should help others less fortunate than herself, and her parents have always encouraged her to get her hands dirty by doing charity work.

Miley does a lot of fundraising for cancer charities because she has been personally affected by the disease. 'My grandad died of lung and prostate cancer, and he was my best friend,' she told *Glamour* magazine. 'I've also lost friends, not just to cancer. My best friend died of cystic fibrosis. It just kills me to see people lose someone they love, so I want to do as much as I can: give money to doctors and hospitals; get nurses in there that care; put a smile on a little kid's face. The things we've done through City of Hope [a centre for cancer research, education and treatment] have been amazing: The Jonas Brothers and I have raised nearly $2.5 million through concerts.'

Miley tried to help raise a similar amount of money for Haiti after the earthquake in January 2010. She sang on two charity singles: 'We Are the World 25 for Haiti' with another 80 big-name stars, and 'Everybody Hurts' with mainly UK artists. Both singles went straight to the top of the music charts and raised a lot of money for the people of Haiti.

Miley might have sung on two singles but she wanted to do more. She organised an online auction on eBay to try and raise even more money. She auctioned off her dress from the Grammy Awards and two tickets to her *The Last Song* premiere, and got other stars involved too. Britney Spears donated her dress from the 2008 MTV Video Music Awards and Nicole Richie donated some jewellery…there were so many stars who wanted to help.

Miley is a real motivator and tries to encourage other people to do their bit for charity. When she was invited to give a short motivational speech before the

Revlon Run/Walk for Women in Los Angeles on 9 May 2009 she jumped at the chance. She told the 50,000 participants: 'Think of all the money that you've raised by working together. And you guys have been doing it sixteen years; that's as old as me. So this is pretty amazing, to have a foundation that has been working for so long and just as many people are here. The Revlon Run/Walk is seriously amazing, so make sure you guys keep it up. We'll keep it going no matter how long it takes, until all of our sisters are safe from these cancers.'

Cheerleading

Miley Cyrus loves cheerleading! She might have been bullied at school but her cheerleading teams have always looked after her and treated her well. She has many friends from her cheerleading days that's she's still in touch with

Miley told *TeenMag*: 'When we would go on trips with my cheerleading team, we would always sing and do karaoke. So I've always been performing.'

Miley was a member of the Premier Tennessee Allstars competitive cheerleading squad and went all over the country competing. She told journalist David Hiltbrand: 'The training is pretty harsh but it's so worth it once you're on stage and getting trophies.' Billy Ray originally wanted Miley to carry on cheerleading before she gave it up so she could concentrate on acting. 'My dad said, "Just stay in school and do cheerleading. Be a normal kid,"' Miley explained.

She had to decide whether she wanted to be a cheerleader or whether she wanted to audition for *Hannah Montana* because her auditions for the show kept conflicting with her cheerleading practice. She might have loved cheerleading but she wanted to be Hannah more.

Miley's mum was a cheerleader and her little sister Noah is now a cheerleader, so it looks like cheerleading runs in the family!

Christmas

Miley loves Christmas. She likes spending time with her family, getting presents, eating good food and most of all…celebrating the birth of Jesus. Miley and her family are Christians and Miley reads the Bible as much as she can.

She told Pete Wentz that Christmas in the Cyrus family is 'Nuts because we've got Trace, who is always on tour who comes in and its like kind of like something new, we're not used to having a rock star in our house…

I'm not as demanding as he is and I take nowhere near as long to get ready, but that's really fun. And we like just being together because it's all about music at Christmas time. Dad sings them [carols].'

Miley had to spend Christmas 2009 in the UK because she was busy performing in the UK in December and January. She was a bit nervous at first because she wasn't celebrating Christmas in the US and she thought the food might be different. She was relieved to find that people in the UK eat turkey too.

Christopher Cody

Christopher Cody is Miley's half-brother. He has the same father as Miley but lives with his mother in South Carolina. Miley and her family rarely mention Christopher in interviews but he does see them occasionally. There are only a few months in age between Miley and Christopher.

Billy Ray is thought to have been dating both Miley and Christopher's mothers at the same time, but after discovering that they were both carrying his baby he decided to marry Tish, Miley's mother, and that he would still financially support Christopher and his mother, and see his son when he could.

Unlike the Cyrus family Christopher doesn't live in

a huge house, and he works in an electronics shop for $7.50 an hour (about £5).

He told the *Mirror* what the real Miley is like: 'She doesn't play the superstar in private. She's a normal teenager having fun and she can laugh at herself. She's the same now as she was before all this fame. She's still my goofy sister. Miley is not a self-obsessed person at all.'

Clothes

Miley loves shopping and trying on new outfits. She usually chooses her own clothes but when she has big award shows coming up she needs an advisor to make sure she wears the right thing.

Despite having millions in the bank, Miley likes picking up bargains when she's out shopping and she'll often mix designer clothing with high-street stuff. She likes clothes that look cool, rather than only picking clothes that have a designer label.

She explained to the *Daily Telegraph*: 'I like to mix it. My favourite store in London is Topshop. I like that you can get kind of more funky things and the prices are very like a wide range. You can get things in there that are like 300 bucks and you can get things in there that are like $8.'

MILEY GLAMMED
UP FOR AN AWARDS
CEREMONY

Miley has so many clothes. Because she is so popular, designers give her clothes for free because they want photographers to snap her wearing their designs. She also has a lot of clothes that she's worn for *Hannah Montana* that she has been allowed to keep, but she regularly picks out some of her best and most memorable outfits to auction off for charity.

Miley thinks her true style would surprise her fans. 'I'm a tomboy! Even though I look all-girlie and act girlie, in reality at home I am such a tomboy. I like to mess around and hang out with my brothers – that is the most fun for me!' she told tribute.ca.

Sometimes she'll enter a store looking rough in a shirt, jeans and pumps and leave with her hair nicely done, wearing a gorgeous dress and heels. Miley believes that looking good makes a big difference when it comes to how she feels about herself. She can't help but smile when she's been on one of those shopping trips.

Miley's mum is usually with her when she shops, so she can keep an eye on what Miley is buying and how much she's spending. In the past, she has wanted Miley to change her style, as Miley explained to interviewers from MuchOnDemand: 'My mom is trying to get me out of [dresses], she's trying to get me to like a rock stage, she's like it goes with your style, it goes with you and I'm like whatever mom I totally like the dresses.' (For this interview Miley was actually wearing the same silver dress the girl who was interviewing her had on!)

Miley's dad isn't bothered how much Miley buys on her shopping trips, but to make her mum feel happier Miley says she's bought outfits for them to share because they are the same size.

Concert

Miley's first concert was one of the most nerve-wracking things she has ever done. She has performed hundreds of times now, but she still gets apprehensive before she goes on stage.

Her first concert was especially tough because the future of *Hannah Montana* rested on how the crowd of 700 kids reacted to her. No one had seen the pilot of *Hannah Montana* yet or had any idea who Miley was – they were just encouraged to go to the free concert and get the chance to appear on TV.

Miley was given just four days to prepare six songs with a singing coach and a choreographer. She couldn't back out and she couldn't have her dad on stage with her; she just had to go out on her own and do her best. She was expecting nothing from the audience except silence – but she was in for a big shock. They loved her!

They chanted 'Hannah, Hannah!' and screamed and chanted for her. It was the same kind of reaction Britney Spears or Beyoncé would get. From that moment on Miley was a star and Disney bosses knew that they had struck gold.

Criticism

Some people enjoy criticising Miley when she makes mistakes. Many fans think this is just because they are jealous of the amazing amount of talent Miley has, and they are jealous of her success.

When Miley posed for the front cover of *Vanity Fair* back in April 2008 the media went crazy saying the image of Miley wrapped in a bed sheet, revealing her bare back, wasn't appropriate. Their cruel words really hurt Miley and her family. She told *Harpers Bazaar*: 'Here, my parents are thinking they're seeing a beautiful picture by a major photographer, and the people of America want to see something dirty in that? It doesn't make sense to us because [my family] doesn't look for negativity. But people don't want to say "What a great performance" or "What a great shot". No one wants to look at something like that and see the positive because it doesn't sell a magazine.'

Some times the media criticises Miley for the way

she dances, or the outfits she wears, as being too provocative. This seems silly to Miley's friends because they know that she's a committed Christian so wouldn't want to be portrayed in that way.

Miley explained her frustration to *Harper's Bazaar*: 'My job is to be a role model, and that's what I want to do, but my job isn't to be a parent. My job isn't to tell your kids how to act or how not to act, because I'm still figuring that out for myself. So to take that away from me is a bit selfish. Your kids are going to make mistakes whether I do or not. That's just life.'

Probably the hardest criticism that Miley has had to face so far has been when reviewers slated her acting skills in *The Last Song*. Miley's fans might have loved the movie but some reviewers were really hard on her. They seem to treat her more harshly than other young actresses her age. Thankfully Miley has her great family, friends and fans to help her through these tough times.

Miley confessed to the BBC: 'I'm a very positive person, I'm super spiritual, and I'm just very connected. If you have a positive mind you'll live a positive life. I surround myself with positivity. I don't really look at the reviews, because I'm very proud of the film. I don't think anyone can really look at the movie and say this film doesn't have a message or this film is useless and was a waste of an hour-and-a-half.

'It's like my music, you don't have to listen to it, you don't have to watch it. Don't ever let anyone ever tell you that something you did isn't good, if you're proud of it.'

D is for...

Dad

Miley's dad, Billy Ray Cyrus, was a very famous singer when Miley was born, performing all over the place to huge audiences. His song 'Achy Breaky Heart' was a huge smash hit all over the world: it was number one in Australia, Canada and the USA. Miley loves the song and likes that people enjoy singing along to it but she finds it 'pretty embarrassing' and would never record her own version of it. She told MTV: 'I think both me and my dad have both heard that song enough. He's the one and only. I don't want anyone to ever cut it, really, because he's the one and only guy that could do it, I think.'

Miley with Billy Ray

When Miley was growing up she was always known as Billy Ray Cyrus's daughter but now people say he's Miley Cyrus's dad. Having a famous dad created problems when Miley was growing up because it made her different, and other kids liked to pick on her because of it. However Miley has inherited her love of performing from her dad. Whenever he was singing onstage Miley would walk on and join in. He can't remember a single performance from when Miley was able to walk that she didn't join him. He loved having her share the limelight with him even when she was a toddler. She wanted his fans to become her fans from a young age. Even then Billy Ray knew that Miley would be a big star. And little Miley never stopped putting on shows for her family to watch – whether they wanted to or not. Miley explained what she was like as a child to BMI.com: 'When I was little, I would stand up on couches and say, "Watch me". We had these showers that are completely glass, and I would lock people in them and make them stay in there and watch me perform. I'd make them watch.'

When Billy Ray's popularity dropped and people started to say he was a one-hit wonder he returned home to the ranch and concentrated on being a dad. He then decided to reinvent himself as an actor and got the lead part in the sitcom *Doc*. In many ways Billy Ray didn't want Miley to follow in his footsteps because he knew how fickle showbiz could be and how people could turn on you in an instant.

Once Miley got the part of Hannah Montana Billy Ray wanted to try out for the part of Robbie Stewart, Miley's dad in the show. He didn't know if he was good enough but he wanted to give it a try. It was the first time he'd considered acting again since his show *Doc*.

Billy Ray told a journalist: 'When I left *Doc* I said I will never do another TV series. I really missed making music and being with my fans…Then this opportunity came up – such a great script, the opportunity to be in business with such a great company as Disney, and then, the icing on the cake, to get to work and experience this with my daughter.'

Billy Ray approached Steve Peterman and the rest of the *Hannah Montana* creators and asked for an audition. They weren't sure at first because they wanted an experienced comedy actor to play Robbie. They knew that Billy Ray hadn't done that much acting before but they decided that it wouldn't do any harm if they gave him an audition because, after all, he was Miley's dad. They weren't expecting anything great but when they compared his audition with the other two dads who had been shortlisted for the part there was one clear winner – Billy Ray. They liked the way Billy Ray and

Miley joked around and interacted with each other, and the fact that he could play the guitar and sing was a huge bonus.

Miley was really pleased when Disney bosses said that Billy Ray would be playing her dad in *Hannah Montana* because it meant that they would be spending a lot of time together. If he hadn't got the part he might have had to live separately from the rest of the family. Having Billy Ray work with her every day made Miley feel loved and protected and she could ask him for advice whenever she needed it.

Working with her dad wasn't all plain sailing. Sometimes he really embarrassed her, as she explained to journalist Maya Motavalli: 'When we're doing photo shoots or something he'll just yell out things I wouldn't want anyone to know. Just random stuff. "Remember that time when you were a kid?" That kind of stuff. But it's funny. It breaks the ice. It makes everyone smile. If it takes embarrassing me to make everyone happy I'll take it.'

When Billy Ray was asked by the *San Francisco Chronicle* about the pros and cons of working so closely with Miley he said: 'It's give and take all the way. It's a fine line, and sometimes it feels like I'm walking it suspended between two of the tallest buildings in New York City. I take one step at a time. Trust me: Whether it's work or personal, sometimes things just get off balance. If I step in the wrong direction, I just try and step back. The most important law is to stay Miley's best friend. We came into this thing as best friends. The most important thing is to keep it that way.'

Miley's dad has been acting for over ten years, so he can help Miley when she's stuck on how to act out a scene. He talked to journalist Delfin Vigil about his acting style and how he decided to become an actor: 'I have been acting so long that I really do feel like an actor. Doing the series *Doc* was like an acting apprenticeship. I found that I liked the less-is-more approach – in a Clint Eastwood kind of way. It's about finding a rhythm to the scene. Being a natural-born musician, the turning point was when I realised that acting was just like making music. My one common law is to keep it real – as a musician and as an actor.'

Billy Ray decided to become an actor after his dad gave him some advice in the mid-1990s. 'He said, "Son, I think you have all your eggs in one basket with this music. I think you should branch out into one of those Kenny Rogers or Dolly Parton careers." The next week, while I was touring in Los Angeles, I read in a newspaper about a casting call for David Lynch's *Mulholland Drive*. My agent helped get me an audition, and lo and behold, they hired me,' Billy Ray revealed.

Billy Ray did so well in *Mulholland Drive* that he got the lead part in the TV show *Doc*. That really made him want to be the best actor he could be, and looking back he thinks that if he hadn't become an actor then Miley might not have either. It was hanging round on the sets of his TV shows that made Miley think that acting would be fun.

Billy Ray likes winding Miley up when they are being interviewed at big events. At the 2009 Academy of Country Music Awards show he was asked by a reporter from Fox News if he ever got sick of Miley. He replied, 'The dress Miley is wearing tonight is perfect, and so are these earrings because they convert into fishing lines real quick.' Miley wasn't pleased with his comments about her earrings and said, 'You've been using this joke forever, and that didn't even make sense, but you just wanted to use it. It's not that funny, you're just upset because I busted you about it. That wasn't even the question; the question was about if you get sick of me and now you're talking about fishing lines. It doesn't make sense – so do you love me or not?'

Sometimes they fall out over silly things but they soon make up. For New Year 2007 they were both supposed to perform on a live show in New York's Times Square but Billy Ray didn't show up. Miley revealed what happened to Yahoo: 'He was mad at me, we got in an argument. He stayed home. It was over a song; I didn't want to do it in a certain key, so he decided to stay at home because it was cold.'

Even when they fall out they still love each other. They have a really close relationship and it makes Miley so upset and angry when she reads internet message boards saying that her dad is using her. Miley says it's the complete opposite: she used her dad to get where she is today. If he hadn't supported her and paid for her to have acting lessons when she was eight she never would have become an actress. Miley always advises budding actors and actresses never to go on message boards when they make a movie just in case something horrible is written on there. She believes the worst comments she has read are the ones that insult her family – because they mean so much to her.

Billy Ray and Miley have achieved so much together. In August 2007 they became the first father and daughter to each have an album in the top 20 since Frank Sinatra and his daughter Nancy. In the future they could break more records.

Dating

Miley is so popular that many boys from around the world would give anything to date her. She is pretty,

MILEY AND LIAM
OUT AND ABOUT

funny and talented and would make anyone the perfect girlfriend. One day she wants to get married and have kids so she is looking for her Mr Right.

Some people might imagine that Billy Ray is quite controlling of Miley and refuses to let her go on dates, but this isn't the case. Miley told *People* magazine: 'He's cool, he's like as long as I make the right decisions then he's pretty cool with it. Not like a hardcore dad, no not at all.'

Miley has dated a few people and two of them have been famous. When she was younger she liked to keep her love life private and it took many months for her to admit that she was dating Nick Jonas from the Jonas Brothers. Things were different when she started going out with Liam Hemsworth, her *The Last Song* co-star. Part of the reason she was happy for people to know that she was dating Liam was that he was happy about going public too.

She revealed to the BBC: 'I've been in relationships before where people don't want people to know because it's bad for their career [but] I'd rather not sneak around – it's so much more drama than is necessary. It's like, "Yes, we're together. Let us live our lives." It's easier because you're not trying to sneak around; otherwise it's news every time you're seen together.'

Miley and Liam did keep their relationship a secret at

first because they were filming *The Last Song* and had to be professional. They didn't tell the director or the rest of the crew but some people probably guessed because Miley and Liam had such great chemistry in the movie.

Miley doesn't really have a 'type' that she goes for because she doesn't judge a book by its cover. She cares about what's in someone's heart and not so much about what they look like (although every guy she's dated has been super hot!). She cares so much about her family that they come as part of the package – if a guy wants to love Miley than he's got to love her family…and her pets.

Miley has been through a lot of pain when her relationships have broken up in the past but she keeps smiling. When she's feeling down she reads her Bible and this helps. After she split from Justin Gaston she tweeted: 'Talking to the one man who keeps his promise. One man who really understands "unconditional love" – Jesus.'

When she's hurting after a split she can always turn to her family for support but sometimes Billy Ray can be a bit harsh with his advice. Miley told *Hello!* magazine what he's like: 'Dad just doesn't get it. He's just like, "Suck it up and get over it! You'll find another one! There's more fish in the sea and he wasn't that good-looking anyway!" He actually did say that once. He's a harsh man to my boyfriends. He's usually cool with them when they're with me…But once it's over – once they dump me or I dump them – then he's always down for bashing them.'

Demi Lovato

Demi Lovato is one of Miley's closest friends. They talk or text each other every day. Demi is a talented actress and singer just like Miley. Demi is most famous for playing Mitchie Torres in the Disney movie *Camp Rock*. She is three months older than Miley and dated Miley's brother Trace for a while.

Demi has given Miley the nickname 'Dragon' because they both love watching the movie *Step Brothers* and like the bit when John C Reilly's character says: 'My name is Dale but you can call me Dragon.'

Demi was really nervous when the paparazzi started following her everywhere but Miley was able to offer her advice and tell her what she should do; she sends Demi lovely text messages to offer her support and help when she needs it most and Demi is really happy to have Miley as a friend.

MILEY WITH DEMI LOVATO

Dolly Parton

The Queen of Country Music Dolly Parton is a close family friend of the Cyrus family, and thinks that Miley has so much talent that she could be a successful actress and singer for many decades to come. She's actually been in a few episodes of *Hannah Montana*, playing the character Aunt Dolly.

Dolly told AOL Music: 'That little Miley Cyrus… she's like a little Elvis! The kids love her because she's Hannah Montana, but what people don't realise about her is she is such a fantastic singer and songwriter. She writes songs like she's 40 years old! She's really deep.

'And I think that she's gonna have a big career after that show [*Hannah Montana*] is off the air. I know I'm partial, because she's my goddaughter. But I'm amazed at the talent that child has and the effect she has on people. And a lot of that ain't just Disney; a lot of that is Miley.'

Dolly has known Billy Ray from before Miley was even born so she was delighted when he asked if she would be Miley's godmother. She comes from a Bible-believing background and feels that famous people like herself, Miley and Billy Ray should use their fame and money for good, believing it's important that they help people less fortunate than themselves.

Miley has been a star from a very young age, and she is always being photographed at premieres and special events.

Miley as Hannah Montana, the character that made her one of the biggest stars in the world.

Miley got her name because she was nicknamed 'Smiley' as a child – you can see why!

Above left: Miley with her mum, Tish, her dad, Billy Ray, and her little sister, Noah.

Above right: Miley signing copies of her album for fans.

Below: Miley with her brother, Trace, and Billy Ray.

Miley always looks amazing whenever she goes to awards ceremonies and parties.

Would you believe these are actually wax models of Miley? She now has waxworks in Madame Tussauds in London and New York, and her fans are almost as excited about meeting them as they are about meeting Miley herself!

Above left: Miley on the set of *Hannah Montana: The Movie*.

Above right: Miley with pop star Katy Perry at the 2008 MTV Video Music Awards.

Below: Miley loves to hang out with family and friends.

Above left: Miley wrapped up warm at the big New York Thanksgiving parade in 2008.

Above right: Miley gets to do all sorts of amazing things, like creating her very own milkshake flavours!

Below left: Miley at the 2008 Oscars.

Below right: Miley performing at New York's famous Rockefeller Plaza.

Driving

In America you can start driving earlier than you can in the UK, so Miley had her first driving lessons when she was fifteen. She didn't find driving as easy as she thought it would be.

She told *TeenHollywood* at the time: 'My driving instructor scares me. We're driving along and he'll say to me, "What's going to happen if you make a left turn?" I'll say, "I dunno" and then he'll go, "Bang – that's going to happen to your brand new car". He just starts hitting things.

'It doesn't help that I have this great big sign on the car saying "student driver". Someone threw a banana at me the other day.'

It's great that Miley worked hard to get her driving licence because, after all, she could have given up and just had a chauffeur drive her around all day. Some celebrities can't handle the pressure of having paparazzi follow them in cars so give up driving. Robert Pattinson, for example, hasn't driven for ages because he doesn't feel safe when they follow him trying desperately to get a photo.

Miley loves her dogs so much that she's had to get a bigger car! When she got her white German Shepherd puppy, Mate, she had to get a bigger car so that he could fit in. She loves the freedom her car gives her and she is forever popping out to see her friends for sushi.

E is for...

Easter Egg Roll

Everyone seems to love Miley, even the President! She was thrilled when she was asked to perform at the White House's Easter Egg Roll in April 2007. She took along her grandmother and her mum because she wanted to share the experience with them and sang on the balcony where President Bush gave his speeches. Since then Miley has been to other Easter Egg Rolls at the Whitehouse and has met the Obama family. She even invited Malia and Sasha to visit her on the *Hannah Montana* set.

Emily Osment

Emily Osment plays Miley's onscreen best friend Lilly Truscott in *Hannah Montana*. She has been acting since she was five and her older brother Hayley Joel is an actor too, with parts in *Forrest Gump*, *The Sixth Sense* and *Pay It Forward*.

The show's creators weren't impressed with Emily when she walked into the audition room for the first time because they thought she looked like she didn't want to be there. She had her hands by her sides and didn't look at all enthusiastic. Once she opened her mouth and started to talk they realised they were wrong – she desperately wanted the part. Emily ended up doing three or four auditions in all before she was told she would be playing Lilly. Miley had already been cast, so her last audition was with Miley to see if they were compatible.

Emily and Miley might play best friends in *Hannah Montana* but they aren't best friends in real life because they have very different personalities; Miley is much closer to Mitchel Musso who plays Oliver Oken. Both Miley and Mitchel are from the country whereas Emily is LA born and bred.

When they were filming seasons 1 and 2 of *Hannah Montana* Miley and Emily would fight and argue with each other, and they didn't hang around with each

MILEY AND EMILY OSMENT

other once the cameras stopped rolling either. Things improved once they filmed *Hannah Montana: The Movie* in Tennessee and they started to get on a lot more during the filming of the third season of *Hannah Montana*.

Miley is very honest about how she gets on with Emily because she wants to be honest with her fans. To begin with both girls had to pretend to be best friends because they were promoting *Hannah Montana*. In a 2008 interview with *Teen Mag* Miley said: 'When we first met, automatically she and I were really, really close. When we're together we're never quiet because there's so much to talk about and there are so many stories. Every day it's something new for us. When you're with someone all the time, it's more than just she and I are friends, we're sisters now. When we first met we had an instant friendship and now we're more like sisters. We love each other like sisters. We fight like sisters. It's always like that.'

When they both turned up at *The Tyra Show* back in 2009 they were wearing almost identical clothes, just in different colours. They were supposed to do mini photo shoots beforehand so it might have been a bit awkward. Back then Miley told Tyra that Emily was her best friend in real life and on the show, but we now know that they aren't that close. It must have been hard pretending to be close to someone you don't get on with. They will never be best friends but they wish each other well.

F is for...

Fame

Miley is one of the most famous girls on the planet right now but it isn't always easy being recognised wherever you go. Miley can't catch up with her friends as much as she would like because she's so busy filming, touring and promoting her latest projects.

Some people feel sorry for Miley because she's been acting since she was very young and has missed out on some of the fun things you go through at school. But although Miley might not have been to her high-school prom she doesn't mind: she had such a horrible time at school being bullied that she was glad to escape.

MILEY HAS HAD TO DEAL WITH BEING PHOTOGRAPHED FROM A YOUNG AGE

She told the BBC: '[You] can't miss what you have never known. I've got to go to the Oscars and meet so many cool people and go to the Grammys and meet the musicians that I like. I would rather do that than stress about whether someone likes my dress or that I don't have a date.'

Having to deal with fame has made Miley very mature for her age. She has had to grow up fast so that people can't take her for granted and push her into things she doesn't want to do. She has had to deal with the press criticising her outfit choices and making comments about her body now that she has grown into a woman. She confessed to the *Boston Globe*: 'It's scary. All of a sudden you're not 4 foot 9 any more and you're not, you know, you're wearing heels and, you know, you've got a body and people just definitely take that into a different aspect.'

Her dad also finds it tough seeing Miley as a superstar. He told the paper: 'I worry about it all the time. Sometimes I think, "Why couldn't everything just be normal? Why couldn't my kids go to a normal school? And why couldn't Miley just be a cheerleader, just be a teenager?"'

Miley feels sorry for celebrity babies because they get photographed and they don't really know what's going on. She thinks its okay for celebrity kids if they want to be famous when they're older like their parents, but until they're old enough to make that decision she believes the paparazzi should stop following them and just let them be babies.

Fans

Miley might have millions of fans now and have signed thousands of autographs but she still remembers meeting her first fan, the day after the *Hannah Montana* pilot aired. She was at an amusement park with her aunt and never expected someone to come over to her and ask for an autograph. Since then, Miley's not stopped signing her autograph and posing for photos with her fans.

When she was being interviewed by the *Daily Telegraph* Miley was asked about the most memorable way a fan had tried to catch her attention. She answered: 'There's a lot. I've been proposed to a few times. You would freak if you saw some of the signs they make sometimes, big flashing signs. It's crazy but it's pretty cool.

'I think they're very creative. It's crazy how creative people get. I'm like, I don't know if I ever loved a star that much, to go through and buy them a ring and everything.'

Miley loves catching up with her fans but sometimes it can be quite scary for her if they all crowd around her and start pushing. When she's at big events she has bodyguards to protect her but when she's just out and about in LA she's on her own. She has to get herself out of tricky situations.

Miley explained to journalist Nicole Berger how she tries to keep her fans happy: 'It's hard 'cause you have to find a balance between keeping everyone happy and also keeping yourself safe, because there's so many people. It's good when you're out and about and there's maybe 10 or 12 people who you want to take a picture with. But not when there becomes 20, 30, 40 people and you're getting lost and you're alone, or you're trying to drive, which in my case is sometimes really hard with paparazzi or fans following. You have to make sure you find the balance, you know, it's important to make your fans happy but also really important to stay safe.'

Sometimes Miley doesn't sign autographs when she's spending time with her family. When they're having meals out together Miley tells fans she can't speak to them right at that moment. She'll speak to them later but not while they're eating.

When she can, Miley likes dropping in on her fans and surprising them. When she was in the UK promoting *Hannah Montana: The Movie* she went to a

London school and surprised all the pupils. She let them ask her anything they wanted and taught them the 'Hoedown Throwdown'. It was an amazing experience for the pupils and something they will never forget.

Miley really appreciates those fans that wait for hours at film premieres just so they can see her for 30 seconds. They make huge posters that declare how great Miley is or how much they love her music. When Miley was younger she didn't have to queue up for hours if she wanted to see a star because her dad almost always knew someone who knew someone. They only people she did queue up for were Hanson brothers, Isaac, Taylor and Zac. Her sister Brandi had a huge crush on the group so Miley went along to keep her company.

Fly on the Wall

'Fly on the Wall' was Miley's favourite track on her *Breakout* album. It only made number 84 on the Billboard Hot 100 in the USA but it did better in other countries. It charted at number 16 in the UK and 23 in Ireland.

Miley loves the 'Fly on the Wall' video because her mum was the one who edited it with her. Miley knew that if she wanted some control over the video, and for it to show the real Miley, she needed her mum to step in and take control. Tish did a great job, with the help of the video's producers Antonina Armato and Tim James of course.

Miley also liked the overall concept of the video, as she explained to Access Hollywood: 'The concept is kind of "Thriller"-esque [sic]. It's kind of like where the paparazzi become these zombies and they're all like attacking me. And my boyfriend is trying to save me, but I don't know if he's a paparazzo too. So, it's like me trying to hide and get away. It's really fun, but I'm escaping from my boyfriend and escaping from the paparazzi and trying to find my way through the whole video.'

Food

Miley loves food, all types from all around the world. She was a bit of a fussy eater when she was younger but that would be difficult now. She has to grab bites to eat when she can and sometimes she only has a few minutes between interviews and has to eat what's available. Some of her favourite foods are pizza (barbecue chicken) and the Spanish dish of eggs with fries. She loves tomato ketchup so much that she drinks it straight from the bottle!

Miley isn't much of a cook but she doesn't have to be

because her mum always makes sure that she's well fed. She can cook a mean breakfast but sometimes she eats random things in the mornings like Doritos and pretzels. She thinks you can eat gross things for breakfast because you have all day to burn it off.

When she asked Liam what her cooking was like after he sampled her pancakes he seemed a bit embarrassed. He told Moviefone that she just sprayed it out of a can so it wasn't really cooking, and even her oatmeal came out of a packet. Miley just laughed and said at least she didn't burn it. Liam and Miley did tend to eat out a lot when they were dating so maybe Miley isn't as good a cook as she likes to think!

When they were filming *The Last Song* they ate out at a restaurant called Stingrays every night and they loved the seafood there. Miley ordered the crabs legs because she liked snapping them, letting all her aggression out in the process. Miley and Liam liked the people too, and Miley even performed there a couple of nights. Liam didn't though, because he's not a singer by any stretch of the imagination.

OPPOSITE: MILEY LOVES FOOD, ESPECIALLY MILKSHAKES!

G is for...

Gary Marsh

Gary Marsh is the Disney Channel's President of Entertainment. He decided a show like *Hannah Montana* had to be made because Disney was making normal kids into huge stars and then once they left Disney they were becoming huge recording artists. People like Britney Spears, Justin Timberlake and Christina Aguilera all started out on Disney shows. Gary told *Variety*: 'We drove these kids into giant success stories…but we thought, "shouldn't we be growing this internally?" We were making celebrities out of other people's rock stars.'

Gary was very involved in the process to find the right girl to play Hannah Montana and he knew Miley desperately wanted to play her after her first audition. He also got his wish of 'growing someone internally': Miley became the first artist to have television, film, consumer products and music deals with Disney.

He explained to *Knight Ridder Newspapers* what made her stand out: 'We got a call from an agent [who said], "Miley will fly herself out to audition again." Let me tell you, we've done a lot of auditions over the years, and no one has ever made that offer before. I said, "We have to see this girl again."'

Hannah Montana fans are so glad Gary made them see Miley again because she was born to play the part. Poor Miley had to fly out for two auditions in the end before she made the shortlist.

Since then Gary has revealed that it was Miley's energy and performance skills that secured her the part. He thinks she's a person who 'loves every minute of life', and has the 'everyday reliability of Hilary Duff and the stage presence of Shania Twain'. She was the girl they waited two years for before they could cast *Hannah Montana*.

He revealed to BMI.com: 'We decided we would not go through with this series until we found a kid who could carry a sitcom as well as she could carry a tune.'

If Miley hadn't come along the show might have never been made.

George Clooney

Miley has a crush on *Ocean's Eleven* actor George Clooney – even though he is the same age as her dad!

Miley was asked which celebrity she had a crush on at the UK premiere of *Hannah Montana: The Movie*. Her fans probably expected her to say Robert Pattinson, Taylor Lautner or maybe Zac Efron, but Miley revealed that it's George Clooney who floats her boat!

Billy Ray didn't seem to be at all surprised that Miley picked George – when he was asked if he was worried that Miley fancied a much older man he said, 'Hey, even I like George Clooney!'

Back then Miley had never dated an actor and vowed to reporters on the purple and yellow carpet that she never would. It was a few months later when she met Liam Hemsworth on *The Last Song* film set that she changed her mind. She must have realised that dating an actor wouldn't be such a bad idea after all.

H is for...

Hands

Miley was born left-handed but her dad tried to teach her to be right-handed. He thought it would be easier on her in the long run. Miley talked about it to Liam Hemsworth in a Moviefone interview: 'I was left-handed when I was younger but my dad was like, "You shouldn't be left-handed... you'll have to learn the world backwards so you need to learn to write with your right hand" and so I started to be right-handed.' Billy Ray is left handed himself and thought it would be easier if Miley learnt how to write with her right hand.

Halfway through her explanation Liam realised she

had already told him – he forgets things Miley tells him sometimes and has to be reminded. He also forgot why her character was called Ronnie in *The Last Song*, even though he'd heard her talk about it in over twenty interviews.

Miley first learnt to play the guitar left-handed and then she decided to learn it right-handed, so now she can do both.

Hannah Montana

Miley's fame to date is all down to her getting cast in the TV show *Hannah Montana*. She wouldn't be the mega star she is today without the Disney show, but on the other hand it was Miley who made the show a big hit. If the casting directors had picked another actress over Miley then the show might have been a huge flop: it was Miley who the audience was able to relate and aspire to.

Miley told the *Daily Mail*: 'When I originally auditioned for the show I was eleven and I didn't get the role till I was thirteen, so it was two years of waiting and wondering if it was ever going to happen for me. It was heartbreaking thinking I wasn't going to get it and my father kept saying: "You know Miles, you've got all the time in the world – take your time and just be a kid", but this was all I ever wanted to do. I wanted to live my dream and I'm just glad everything's finally worked out.'

Once she got the part the hard work really started. She had to develop two characters, learn how to go from one to the other quickly and learn loads of lines. She explained what it was like playing dual roles to TV critic David Kronke:

'As an actor, it's really fun, because you get to experience different things from different perspectives. As a person, it's a little harder. It's double the work – not only for me but for the wardrobe people, the hair and make-up people and everyone else. It's hard but really fun to be the character.

'The cool part is I've gotten to add my own take to it. I relate to both of them so easily. I take the script in, but it's important to be myself. I didn't want to make a big fake persona, because the script calls for a real girl. So, my being from Tennessee with no experience worked to my advantage – they got the normal, average girl and turned me into a pop star.'

Hannah Montana premiered on 24 March 2006 to the largest audience ever recorded for a Disney Channel show – 5.4 million people tuned in, and each week after that the buzz around the show kept building. Kids couldn't get enough of Hannah Montana!

Miley enjoys watching old episodes and seeing the thirteen-year-old version of herself. She can watch the first season and remember lots of things that happened to her in real life that were written into the show. Other times she would film an episode about something and the very next day it would happen to her in real life. How weird.

Miley's fans were shocked when she decided that she wanted to say goodbye to *Hannah Montana* and that the fourth season would be the last. They didn't really want the show to come to an end but Miley wanted a new adventure. She liked the security the show gave her but she wanted to break out of the routine of working 8.30–6pm every day on the *Hannah Montana* set.

She explained to *People* magazine: 'I'm a little nervous because now it's like I don't have something to fall back on. But I'm getting excited. I think a lot of pressure is going to be taken off of me. I'm not going to be tied down to a company where they're like, "She sings! She acts!" I can choose when I want to do music and when to do movies. I won't have this mould they want me to fit into. I can just be what I want to be.'

Miley also feels that leaving *Hannah Montana* behind her will be a good thing because she's not the same little girl she was when she first got the part. She doesn't want to be really famous and be recognised all the time like she did when she was thirteen. She has other priorities now and just wants to have fun and enjoy what she does every day. Sometimes she didn't enjoy filming *Hannah Montana* but she couldn't stop and take a day off because people needed her there and it would have messed up the filming schedule.

Now that *Hannah Montana* is ending Miley is really giving the opportunity to another young actress to be the next big Disney star, as the studio will no doubt come up with an idea for another hit show that Miley's fans can also enjoy.

She will miss the cast and crew from her *Hannah Montana* days but probably not the *Hannah Montana* dolls, bedding, lunch boxes and the thousands of other items with her face on them. As she said to *Parade* magazine: 'I am not a doll, and people want to treat me that way. I'm older now. I have an opinion. I have my own taste.' Miley will also like the freedom to wear what she wants everyday and not what the wardrobe department picked for her to wear.

When Miley made the decision to quit *Hannah Montana* it was the end of the road for all the actors and actresses on the show as they couldn't carry on without Miley. They all had to think about their futures and what they wanted to do next. Billy Ray knew before the others because he's Miley's dad, but he didn't try

and change her mind. He told *People* magazine: 'I've gotten to go through this entire journey with Miley and watch her grow not only as a little girl to a young lady but as an actress. For any daddy out there to get to go through that with one of their children, it's an amazing journey.'

Miley has so many fond memories of filming the four seasons of *Hannah Montana* and will never forget the friends she has made. She is going to take some of her outfits and her wig and frame them so there is a permanent reminder of *Hannah Montana* on her wall back home.

Hannah Montana & Miley Cyrus: Best of Both Worlds Concert 3-D

Miley did her first tour from 18 October 2007 to 3 January 2008. It was called the Best of Both Worlds tour and was a huge success. Sadly for many fans they couldn't get to see Miley because ticket touts snapped up lots of the tickets and sold them for five times their original price. There was also such a demand that venues sold out within a few minutes, so lots of genuine fans were left feeling very disappointed.

Miley hated seeing her fans upset so decided to make *Hannah Montana & Miley Cyrus: Best of Both Worlds Concert 3D*, a film of the concert that fans could go and watch in their local cinemas (and later buy on DVD). Miley divulged to the *Baltimore Sun*: 'It was kind of like a 3D reality show. It was wild, having them follow you around with their cameras and, you know, me and someone would get in an argument or something bad would happen, and they would run up and be like, "Can I mike you?" And it's like, "Aw, come on."'

Miley was really passionate about doing the concert in 3D for the fans who couldn't be there, as she explained to the Associated Press: '[We did it] mostly because of the tickets and there were so many people that didn't get to come to the show. This is like better than front row. You could reach out and feel like you could touch my hand you could see me right then. Right there, right in front of you, which is so fun. Also just to be able to see behind the scenes, which I think is the most clever part of anything. Just getting to see what goes into this. They can walk around knowing what real hard work it is. I mean I think I have the easiest job.'

Hannah Montana: The Movie

As well as there being several *Hannah Montana* TV series, concerts and a 3D concert movie, Miley got to be in *Hannah Montana: The Movie*. It was the first movie

MILEY PERFORMING AS
HANNAH MONTANA

MILEY ON THE SET OF *HANNAH MONTANA: THE MOVIE*

that Miley had acted in where she had more than a handful of lines (she had previously played a little girl called Ruthie in *Big Fish*). She had voiced Penny in the animated movie *Bolt*, but this was definitely a bigger deal as she would be onscreen in nearly every scene.

The movie was a huge success right from the word go and was number 1 in the box-office chart on its opening weekend, making a massive $34 million in ticket sales! Its premiere in Nashville drew huge crowds as fans waited for hours for the opportunity to see Miley. Miley was joined by her dad, her close friend Taylor Swift and lots more stars from the movie.

Miley and Billy Ray were so glad that the movie was shot in Tennessee, where they are from. They liked the fact that the audience would see how beautiful the landscape and people of Tennessee are. Originally it was going to be shot somewhere else, which upset Billy Ray and so he flew back home and took as many photos of the surroundings as he could to prove to everyone that the movie had to be filmed there. The producers were so impressed with the filming locations that Billy Ray found that they changed their minds and set about arranging for the movie to be shot in Tennessee as originally planned. This really helped the Tennessee film industry and created a lot of jobs for people in the area.

Miley told CNN: '[Filming the movie] actually gave me time to relax, and it was when my career was just starting to take off…when I was just starting to travel. It was at a time when I needed to go back home and it couldn't have been more of a perfect time.'

This mirrored what happened to Miley Stewart in the movie. She is forced to go back home and has to decide what she really wants: to be famous or to be a normal girl.

Billy Ray explained to the reporter: 'This is definitely an example of art imitating life imitating art… It's so important to be aware of where you're at and be focused on where you're going but, more importantly, never forget where you came from. You can't fake going home. That was her home.'

Both Miley and Billy Ray are really happy with the way the movie turned out. They were able to show even more of their real-life closeness, as Miley's dad explained to the *San Francisco Chronicle*: 'The movie itself is as close to real life as it can be, while still keeping the comedy and the whole stuff that makes the *Hannah Montana* series work. Even down to the song I sing, "Back to Tennessee". That becomes the theme of the movie and the cornerstone of the film. The words and lyrics are about living there and knowing we both had to go home. My dad had this saying: "Always look toward the future, but most importantly, never forget where you came from and who you are." And that's what this movie and the song are about.'

Heart condition

You can't tell from looking at Miley but she has a heart condition. She didn't realise anything was wrong until she felt ill during her Best of Both Worlds tour. She went to get herself checked out and was told that she had a hole in her heart and a condition called tachycardia.

People with tachycardia have heart rates that exceed the normal range for a resting heartbeat. It means that their hearts are pumping faster so blood is pumped less efficiently, which means that their bodies receive less blood than they need. This can make the person feel ill, and struggle to breathe if they do too much.

Miley just has to watch now that she doesn't push herself too hard when she's performing and that she doesn't overheat when she's wearing Hannah Montana's wig. Doctors aren't worried as this condition isn't life threatening for Miley.

During an interview with *Xposé* Miley tried to give her interviewer who had the same heart condition some advice about dealing with stress. She told her: 'I always just try to think, step away from the situation and put yourself ten years from where you are now and then say, "Alright is this really going to be significant in my life? Is this going to change where I'm going to be in ten years? At my happiest moment is this going to be weighing on my mind…no". Otherwise I'll just OCD myself to death. I'll be like I have to call, I have to fix dinner… finally it's like, it'll all work out.'

Holidays

Miley loves going on holiday with her family when she gets the chance. She's been to so many places promoting her TV series, movies and music that people wrongly think she's seen the world many times over, but she hasn't. She's always so busy that she's flown from one country to the next, whisked from one interview to the next, sleeps in hotels and then is sent the next day to a new location. She doesn't have time to sightsee or explore places properly. It's only when she's on holiday that she can do this properly, and she doesn't get the chance to go on that many holidays because she's so busy all the time.

The *Daily Telegraph* recently asked Miley what had been her best holiday destination. She replied: 'I think it's anywhere where you can escape, you know, where not a lot of people are. I went to Los Cabo in Mexico with my mum and I loved that, it was so much fun. We had a good time just me and my mum.

'We were totally alone, we were very secluded which was great. I think that's the best part about vacation is just not having to put make-up on, not having to look great, like I can just do whatever.'

Sometimes Miley can't escape the paparazzi and even though she can't see them they can see her. They have very powerful cameras that can take photos from far away but look like they've been stood right next to her when they've taken them. It must be frustrating for Miley's mum and dad when people spy on Miley and take photos of her in her bikini.

Home

They say that home is where the heart is and this is true for Miley. Her first home was a 500-acre farm in Tennessee, but she has moved around a lot since then. When she was eight the whole Cyrus family moved to Toronto in Canada because Billy Ray was acting in the TV series *Doc*. They had to all move again when Miley was cast in *Hannah Montana* because she had to be based in Los Angeles.

Miley's mum picked their first Los Angeles home

MILEY TAKES A BREAK
FROM FILMING TO
PLAY ON THE BEACH

off the internet and bought it without even viewing it. She just liked the photos on the website and knew it would be a nice place to live. She didn't have time to spend looking at various properties; she just needed somewhere the Cyrus family could move straight into.

When Miley was about to tour for the first time Miley's mum decided that she needed to buy Miley her own bus. She didn't want Miley to have to share a bus with all her dancers who were a lot older than her. Miley's bus was a chilled-out home from home. Miley could shut the door and be little Miley again and not a big star. She shared it with her mum Tish, her grandmother, her little sister Noah and her dogs. It was perfect.

Miley loves living with her family but from being a young teenager she has always wanted her independence. She has always said that her mum made her promise to live at home until she was twenty, but she recently admitted that she got out of it. She's bought her first home and is excited about decorating it how she likes. It's only a few doors away from her parent's home so she'll always be able to pop back whenever she wants and they'll be able to keep an eye on her. No doubt her little sis Noah will be planning to sleep over a lot.

It's thought that Miley's first house cost a massive $3.4 million to buy. It has four bedrooms, lots of bathrooms, a swimming pool and a tennis court. It has its very own recording studio and a separate guest building with two more bedrooms.

Liam Hemsworth joked to *People* magazine that he's going to help her decorate: 'I could come in and gather some pictures of myself to put on her wall and see what she says. I'll sign it for her as well, and it will say, "Dear Miley, best wishes with the new house!"'

Joking aside, Miley is going to get a lot of help from her mum Tish. She explained to *People* magazine: 'My house is going to be gorgeous because my mom is an interior designer. It's like if your mom's a clothes designer you're always going to look great. My mom's an interior designer so my house is going to be perfect all the time.'

They've decided that the house will be really informal with cool low-seater couches and huge cushions on the floor so Miley and her friends can just chill out. She's making her house open to all her friends so they can come and visit whenever they want. That way she'll never be lonely.

Hospitals

Some people have a real phobia of visiting hospitals but not Miley. She has been taking presents to sick people in hospitals since she was very small. When her dad was performing his big hit 'Achy Breaky Heart' he would receive lots of flowers and gifts from fans. but instead of keeping them all to himself he would give them to people in hospital. Miley really liked going with her dad and with members of her church to show ill people that they loved them.

Visiting people in hospital really helps Miley keep things in perspective. When fame is getting too much she can drop in and make someone's day. It helps her realise that she has nothing to complain about. She is healthy and free to go wherever she wants; some of the patients she visits don't have that luxury and are very sick.

When Miley is touring or in foreign countries she doesn't forget her friends in hospital. She makes sure that she gives them a phone call or two to let them know she's thinking of them – she's a great role model.

I is for...

Inspiration

Millions of people might look to Miley for inspiration but for Miley it's people like Kelly Clarkson and Hilary Duff who inspire her to do what she is doing. When she's acting, Miley doesn't try and copy anyone else, she just tries to be true to herself and let her own personality shine through the characters she plays.

When Miley was asked by *Glamour* who her role models were, she said: 'This is actually funny. I'm a huge Jennifer Aniston fan and a huge Angelina Jolie fan. Jennifer Aniston can put on a plain black dress, with plain make-up and hair, and look so stunning. Angelina always looks so comfortable in her own skin: At a premiere she was wearing a pantsuit – what woman throws that on and looks smoking hot? She's also changed every couple of years, going from wild child to being a mom and having a normal life. And Jennifer Aniston bounced back after her divorce. She could have gone crazy with so many different guys, but she didn't. If anything like that ever happens to me, I'm like, Pull a Jennifer, Miley! She is so classy.'

In the future Miley would like the opportunity to be in a movie with Jennifer Aniston, Hilary Duff and *Transformers*' star Shia LaBeouf.

Hilary Duff is probably the person who has inspired Miley the most because she was the first big Disney star and paved the way for Miley to follow. Hilary had Lizzie Maguire and Miley had Hannah Montana. They can both act and sing and share many of the same character traits.

When MTV asked Miley if she looked up to Hilary in particular, she replied, 'Yeah, because she's on Disney, or was on Disney Channel, and she's kind of set the way for all of us, not only just in a business sense, but [by] saying that it is OK to be a good girl. Like, that's cool! It's kind of just given us all inspiration to go out. Whether it was her or not, I would definitely be doing what I'm doing, but she definitely made it more acceptable.

'For sure [I want to have a career like hers]. I wanna do it my own way, and I have different ways. [But] she's very vocal about it as well. She likes going out and talking about being a good role model. [Similarly] in the things I do, like a 3D movie, where you get to see that it's not fake, it's not just being at an interview and saying, "Yeah, I wanna be a good girl". It's really showing you making right decisions in the movie.'

Miley isn't best friends with Hilary or anything, but the older performer has offered Miley advice in the past. She has told Miley to remember on bad days why she wants to perform – that it's the thrill of making young girls happy and not the 'being famous and making lots of money' part. She told Miley to cling on to the positives all the time and not think about the negatives.

Another actress that Miley rates is Sandra Bullock. She explained why she loves Sandra Bullock to VH1: 'I think she does a little bit of everything, she's hilarious, she can make me cry, she can make me laugh…she does a little bit of everything.'

Internet

The internet can be a great tool for Miley fans as it allows them to chat to each other in forums and read all the latest news on Miley. She regularly blogs on her official site and posts cool YouTube videos too. Sometimes when fans spot Miley out and about in Los Angeles they tweet about it so other fans can come and meet her too.

On occasion the internet isn't so great, though, and poor Miley has had to put up with lots of bloggers and media people writing nasty things about her. They have posted some cruel things that must be really upsetting for Miley and her family to read.

Perez Hilton has been one of the worst offenders and doesn't seem to be able to stop writing horrible things about our favourite star. Miley has been so upset by what he has written in the past that she has talked to the *Daily Mail* about it: 'That can be painful. That's just a mean person. I don't know how old he is, but taking it out on me is a little strange. It's like going back to high school. I get to travel and go to London and Paris, while this person sits by the computer writing mean things about me. I'd rather be the one travelling.'

Miley did have a Twitter account for a long time and it was really popular (she had two-million followers) but she decided to stop after she received hate messages from people who disagreed with her views. She decided to write a rap about why she was leaving the site and posted it on YouTube. Check out the 'Good-bye Twitter' video – it's really funny and the lyrics are powerful and explain how Miley is feeling. In her rap Miley says that she's not leaving because Liam Hemsworth told her to but because she was tweeting about pimples and things that didn't matter. She realised that people didn't need to know when she was playing with Noah or brushing her hair. She says she's about to turn over a new leaf and start living for the moment, not for the tweets. She was also sick of gossip sites analysing every tweet and acting like it was news. She wanted her private life to be private again. Miley proves how talented a songwriter she is in this rap, which has been viewed over 11 million times. Her friends joined in the fun music video which is filmed in a girls' bathroom and a rehearsal room. They dance about in sunglasses while Miley does her best rapper impression.

Miley might like talking to her friends online but she avoids message boards. She admits she would probably like them if the comments were about someone else but it's hard when she sees page after page of negative stuff about her. One day things got too much for Miley and she replied to a nasty message pretending to be one of her own friends from Nashville. She told the person that they were the biggest jerk and what they had written wasn't true. She said they were a horrible person but ended up deleting her message because she felt terrible. Miley never likes to be mean.

Interviews

Miley has done thousands of interviews so it must be quite tiresome when she gets asked the same questions again and again. Her best interviews are the ones where fans ask the questions, because they always ask interesting questions.

Sometimes Miley has to rush from one interview to the next and mistakes happen. During one radio interview when she was speaking on the phone she was cut off because their time had run out and transferred to the next radio station. She received a lot of criticism because people thought she'd done it on purpose to avoid talking about Jamie Foxx. He'd made some nasty comments about her when he was trying to be funny, and the presenter had just asked Miley about it when the line went dead.

Miley explained what happened via her twitter account. 'There's a little drama (of course the world loves it ew) because apparently I "hung up" on radio stations today and I hate to say that's not true. I have a specific time limit and schedules are set up for specific time frames for each station…if a station goes over time I am IMMEDIATELY connected to the next station. YES, i am sorry if anyone thought I "hung up" on them. The peeps at the radio stations r friends we know each other well and have a great relationship. I'm sorry if anything was miscommunicated, taken out of context, or misunderstood. xo'.

Iron Maiden

Many people think that Miley only likes pop music but she actually likes lots of different music styles. She is a big fan of Iron Maiden and loves wearing her Iron Maiden top. When she first started wearing it out and about in January 2009 some people were really judgmental and said she was only wearing the top to pretend to be cool. This couldn't have been further from the truth – Miley is a massive Iron Maiden fan.

She never likes her fans to get the wrong impression of her so recorded a special video for them and put it on YouTube. In it she said, 'I'm sure you all have seen me rocking an Iron Maiden shirt lately and I know there's been some people saying, "Oh, she's a poser" and

"The only reason she's wearing Iron Maiden is because she wants to be a rock star."

'So, Iron Maiden – "Run To The Hills", "Fear of the Dark", "Running Free", [all] good song[s], check it out. So thank you, guys. I actually do like Iron Maiden.'

J is for...

Jason Earles

Jason plays Miley's brother Jackson Stewart in *Hannah Montana*. He has known Miley since 2006 when they started filming *Hannah Montana*. Before then, he'd been in a few TV shows and movies including *MADtv*, *National Treasure* and *American Pie Presents Band Camp*.

When Jason was first cast as Jackson the creators thought he should have a ventriloquist dummy in the show so he could say things he wouldn't naturally say. They thought it would enable him to express how Jackson feels about his sister being a star. When they saw Jason perform with the dummy they thought it was

Jason Earles

really funny but that Jason was so good at comedy that he didn't need a dummy. They ended up scraping the dummy and keeping Jason.

Jason is a bit of a mystery because no one knows his exact age. It is thought that he is around 33 years old but his acting CV has him eight years younger than that. He always plays characters a lot younger than himself because of his youthful appearance. He has two cats and an Australian Shepherd dog called Andy. Like Miley, he loves horse riding.

Jason started acting at school in Oregon and the first play he was in was *Hansel and Gretel*. He moved to California and started going to castings in the hope of becoming an actor.

Jason loves acting alongside Miley and gets on really well with her dad. He told *Portrait* magazine about his best *Hannah Montana* moment: 'I'll never forget the episode where Billy Ray and I were pranking each other and he tricked me into running through a door and falling into a pool of pudding! I'm supposed to just come crawling out of the door, dripping in pudding and say, oh you got me good dad! But Billy Ray and I like to improve and do extra stuff on the scenes so I started to chase him through the set like I was going to hug him because I was covered in pudding, and as I am running and chasing him out of the room of the kitchen, I slip and fall on my butt really hard... Everyone thought it was so funny that it ended up being in the show! If you watch the fall on the show, it hurts! It was a big fall!'

When he gets covered in gunk he heads to his dressing room – all the stars on *Hannah Montana* have one, although Miley's is the nicest. Jason told *Portrait* magazine about his dressing room: 'It's actually cool! I call it the dirty dorm room! I bring my PlayStation in there and it's got my guitar, which I'm terrible at playing, pillows, blankets, we have a little bathroom attached to it with a shower so that when they get me all messy on the show by throwing pudding at me for example, I pop in and clean myself! It's a pretty comfortable room. It has a couch, a couple of chairs, a little table, a small TV! It works!'

Jason thinks that a lot of the boys who made guest appearances in episodes of *Hannah Montana* had big crushes on Miley. He is happily married to his wife Jennifer and says the only woman he had a crush on when she visited the set was Dolly Parton.

Jason has become a member of the Cyrus family in many ways because they spend so much time together and they will always stay in touch. Before they shot the pilot he was quite nervous because he knew he would be joining a real dad and a real daughter. He said in an interview with TheStarScoop.com: 'I was really worried about it at first, but anybody that's spent any time around Billy Ray and Miley, they quickly feel right at ease. What you see is what you get. They're very accepting of new people and new experiences. They just sort of embraced me as part of the family from the very beginning. They did a great job of even extending that beyond me. Oliver and Lily, the two best friends, they were just as readily accepted into the whole Cyrus clan as I was. I think it's really a sort of testament to them starting off on the right foot, letting the chemistry just be as opposed to making it awkward at first.'

Jason thinks people would be surprised at what him and Miley get up to when the cameras stop rolling.

'She's sort of like – and don't take this the wrong way, I hope she doesn't take this the wrong way – she's sort of like hanging out with a dude. You can't say anything to shock her. We spend more time burping and farting around each other on the set – I think people would be just shocked with how non-shockable she is.'

He added to WZAP Radio: 'She's also cool to just joke around with. We play a lot of *Guitar Hero* in her dressing room. When we have breaks, we run out and get sushi together.'

Jason, Miley and the rest of the *Hannah Montana* cast tended to joke around on Mondays, Tuesdays and

Wednesdays because these were the days they rehearsed their scenes. On Thursdays and Fridays they couldn't afford to mess around because they were filming so they all had to act professionally and maintain their focus.

Jesus

Jesus is the number one man in Miley's life and always will be. She loves talking about her faith and would love it if she inspired her fans to pick up a Bible and get to know him.

She might not be a preacher like her great-grandfather but she wants to be a light in the darkness. Her dad is a strong Christian too and echoed Miley's beliefs when he told *Today's Christian* magazine: 'I am at peace with my life – past, present and future. I know all things that are good come from Almighty God above. I count my blessings every single day. Every day I pray God will show me the doors He wants me to walk through, the people He wants me to talk to, the songs He wants me to sing. I want to be the light He wants me to be in this world.'

Miley echoed his thoughts when she spoke to FOX News: 'I think it's my faith that keeps me grounded, especially because I'm a Christ follower, for sure. Live like Christ and he'll live in you, and that's what I want to do.'

Miley and her family go to church every Sunday and then spend the rest of the day chilling out together. Miley knows that being a Christian is more than just going church on a Sunday: she tries to pray and read her Bible every day. At first Miley and her family just went to church because they liked it; they didn't have a relationship with Jesus. This changed when they joined The People's Church in Franklin. Suddenly things slotted into place and they started to put God first in their lives.

Jodie Foster

Jodie Foster is a very experienced actress who has picked up two Oscars and is best known for playing Clarice Starling in *The Silence of the Lambs*. She has been acting since she was three and so knows exactly what Miley's going through. Jodie has called and given Miley advice and Miley knows that if she ever needs help dealing with a situation she can always contact Jodie.

Miley confessed to the *Daily Mail*: 'It's hard growing up in the spotlight and I'm changing. I can't be the twelve-year-old who just moved to LA for ever. I'm having a great time doing what I do, but I'm also going to stumble and fall. Having my parents close helps. People mention child performers who have gone off the rails, but there are also stable people like Jodie Foster. She was a child star and look where she is now.'

It would be great if one day Miley could be in a movie with Jodie, to work with the Oscar winner and learn all she can from her. And maybe one day Miley will win her own Oscar!

Jonas Brothers

Miley is forever being linked with the Jonas Brothers because she went out with Nick Jonas for a couple of years, and they all toured together.

When she was being interviewed on the *Ellen DeGeneres Show* while they were touring together, Miley was asked who her favourite Jonas was. She told Ellen that Nick was her favourite because he's 'cute'. A few weeks later the Jonas Brothers were on Ellen's show and a fan asked whether Miley was Nick's favourite. He replied, 'No, she's a cool girl, I think we're just enjoying each other's company on the road right now and having fun.'

Ouch. Poor Miley. For ages they tried to keep their relationship a secret by saying they were just good friends. When they split things went nasty for a while but they are back being good friends now. They might have dated when they were only twelve but Miley believes

NICK JONAS

that they were both very mature because they were growing up in show business and had albums and shows to promote all the time. They each wanted to be the best performers they could, and wanted their records to do really, really well. It was tough with them both being big stars because one day she would be in Germany, the next Nick would be somewhere else…so it was difficult for them to be in the same place at the same time and to be able to chill out together without the interruption of work commitments. Nick will always be Miley's first love and she says she will always love him with all of her being. Any potential boyfriends will have to be aware that she quite often texts Nick to let him know what she's up to.

In April 2009 Miley had to tell the press that they weren't back together after they were snapped having lunch. Gossip sites started saying they were dating again but that wasn't the case at all. Miley told journalists: 'We aren't back together. I don't think people know how to make an ex-boyfriend into a best friend and it seems impossible. But when you have known each other as long as we have – we did have such a great relationship. Even he has said, "We don't know what will happen in the future but for right now, we know we are best friends."'

It's not known how Miley's parents feel about her

being friends with Nick, but they are the forgiving type so they probably don't feel any resentment or anger. That said it must have been awful for Tish to have to help her daughter mend her broken heart.

'Going through that with your daughter is really, really hard, especially for Miley being on tour,' she told *E!* 'There were times when I was like, "Oh my gosh, I just wish we were home and she could just kind of get over this in private."'

Miley decided to be honest with her fans and let them know how she was feeling during the weeks that followed her split from Nick. She was able to show them that just because a relationship breaks down it doesn't mean that you'll never be happy again. Miley cried for a month and dyed her hair black to rebel against Nick because he liked her hair just the way it was. Now it probably seems silly but back then it allowed Miley to move forwards.

She revealed all about their romance to *Seventeen* magazine: 'We became boyfriend and girlfriend the day we met. He was on a quest to meet me, and he was like, "I think you're beautiful and I really like you." And I was like, "Oh, my gosh, I like you so much."

'For two years he was basically my 24/7. But it was really hard to keep it from people. We were arguing a lot, and it really wasn't fun.'

Because Nick is famous too and was tied to Disney, Miley wasn't able to completely cut him out of her life and this probably helped her stay friends with him.

Josh Duhamel

The *Transformers* actor Josh Duhamel might be married to Black Eyed Peas singer Fergie, but that didn't stop Miley winding him up on a flight from Los Angeles to London. She found out that she could send text messages to other passengers on the flight via their seats, so sent Josh a few cheeky messages. She called up Ryan Seacrest's radio show to tell him all about it: 'I was, like, "Hey stud!" He didn't know which seat I was in, so I could tell him all these funny things [without being discovered]. He didn't text me back [because] it was rude.'

Miley loves messing around, but it might have been embarrassing if she'd bumped into Fergie!

Julie Anne Robinson

Miley left a lasting impression on Julie Anne Robinson, the director of *The Last Song*. She thinks that Miley has real potential and could be the next Julia Roberts. The director of photography on the movie feels the same.

He has worked with Julia Roberts in the past and thinks they are very similar.

Julie told *E! Online*: 'She's like Julia Roberts. I feel Miley can do anything – action, comedy, drama. She's got it all.'

Before Miley was cast, Julie hadn't met her before or seen *Hannah Montana* but she knew she was perfect for the lead role. The only problem was that she was so much smaller than Liam Hemsworth. When they needed to shoot one scene where Miley stands behind him they couldn't do it because she was too small. Julie had Liam stand in a hole and this made Miley look taller and they were able to shoot the scene as they wanted.

Miley loved working with Julie: 'If you don't really bond with the director, I think it comes across on screen. Julie Anne was so much fun. She went above and beyond to create a bond. It was important to me that she had confidence in me,' she said.

Justin Bieber

Miley is good friends with 'Baby' hit-maker Justin Bieber, but nothing more, despite what the gossip sites say. They've been out for dinner together and hung out but he is way too young for Miley.

MILEY WITH EX-BOYFRIEND JUSTIN GASTON

Miley's little sister Noah has a huge crush on Justin, but Miley knows he has 10 million girls who want to date him. If he did happen to fancy her, though, Miley would be flattered even though she says he's like a brother to her.

He can be very annoying sometimes and will text Miley in the middle of the night and wake her up just to wind her up. Miley hates it when he does this but she still thinks he's adorable. Miley has even admitted in an interview that Justin is her 'travel-size boyfriend'!

Justin Gaston

When Miley was sixteen she dated underwear model Justin Gaston. He was four years older than her so some people said he was too old. Miley's parents disagreed; they really liked Justin and thought he was a good influence on Miley.

When they were dating Miley announced on *The Rachael Ray Show*: 'I've never been closer to the Lord since I met him. He's really made me read my Bible. He's made me actually read the stories in the Bible – not the quick little verses – that not only help me, but show you how to help other people.'

Miley didn't fall head over heels in love with Justin straight away; in fact she walked straight past him! It was her dad who introduced her to Justin when they were on the *Hannah Montana* set. They became good friends first and then she realised how cute he was.

When they split Miley's fans were surprised because they'd seemed so happy together but Miley explained that she had to end it because having a long-distance relationship wasn't working out for them.

K is for...

Kelly Preston

Kelly Preston is the actress who plays Miley's mum in the movie *The Last Song*. Kelly is married to John Travolta and they are personal friends of the Cyrus family.

Miley was the one who approached Kelly and asked her to be in the movie. Kelly and John had only lost their son Jett a few months before, but Kelly felt that the time might be right to act again once Miley asked her.

She told *People* magazine she did it 'because Miley asked me herself to play her mom. I was really moved. It was the perfect movie to sort of get my feet wet.'

Kelly's daughter was thrilled because she's a big Miley fan and got to hang around the set. Even though both families had been friends for a while, it was during the filming of *The Last Song* that they got super-close.

Kissing

Miley's first kiss ever was on the set of *Hannah Montana*. She was really nervous because she'd never done it before, but the boy she had to kiss mistook her nerves and thought she was nervous because she might be a bad kisser. She never names him in interviews but says that he taught her how to kiss. After the cameras stopped rolling she said bye and ran off. It must have been weird having to share your first kiss with a room full of people.

Miley has had quite a few on-screen kisses. When she was filming *Hannah Montana* she never got to pick who she was going to kiss; she was just told who her love interests were going to be. You would have thought she'd have been embarrassed kissing boys with her dad nearby but she wasn't. She sees on-screen kisses as being part of the job and not the same as kissing boys in real life.

When Miley had to kiss Lucas Till in *Hannah Montana: The Movie* it might have been hard for her boyfriend at the time, Justine Gaston, to watch but she didn't have a problem with it.

She told reporters: 'He's seen the movie, and it's only acting, so I guess you have got to keep that in your mind. And I'm sure it's probably a little hard, but we're actors. We have got to be good at our jobs.'

Lucas was really happy that he got to work with Miley and he told CNN: 'She's really nice and really [endearing], and she really cares about people. She's a good friend, very loyal.' He also hinted that 'there was a lot more there to that kiss than you see.' When Miley was asked whether Lucas was a good kisser she replied, 'Meh, he's OK. No, I'm just kidding. I don't know. I think I was too busy thinking about my next line to think about it.'

Kissing Liam Hemsworth for the first time on the set of *The Last Song* was strange because it was their first day on set and they hardly knew each other to talk to let alone kiss. Liam explained to Ryan Seacrest: 'We turned up on set the very first day and originally it was just a scene where we were running through the water and splashing and having fun. And halfway through the scene, the director, Julie Anne, she yelled "Kiss!" And we got thrown into a kiss on the boat. It was good, 'cause, you know, [you] get the first one out of the way, and it was fine.'

It must have been strange a few weeks later when they were dating and had to kiss in character. Those kisses most have been more than just work for Miley.

L is for...

Lesley Patterson

Lesley Patterson is Miley's best friend from back home in Nashville, while Mandy Jiroux is Miley's best friend from LA. Lesley has known Miley for a very long time and they used to be in the same cheerleading squad.

Lesley told Philly.com: 'Ever since I've known her she's always been singing non-stop. My mom used to tell her, "Girl, you're going places".' Lesley's mum is one of Dolly Parton's personal assistants so she knows talent when she sees it.

Lesley has become a big celebrity in the cheerleading circuit simply for being Miley's best friend. People come up to her and ask for her autograph. At a huge cheerleading competition in 2008 Lesley was called on stage so people could see what Miley's best friend looked like. Poor Lesley looked so nervous as she made her way to the front. They were hundreds of people there, all staring at her!

Miley showed the world how much Lesley meant to her in her song 'See You Again'. Miley's other best friend wasn't upset that Miley mentioned Lesley in the song instead of her. Mandy understands that Miley has been close to Lesley for years and that she is her Nashville best friend. Mandy's just glad that she gets to see Miley a lot because they both live In LA most of the time.

Liam Hemsworth

We'll have to wait and see if actor Liam is 'the one' for Miley. They might be complete opposites but they got on so well when they were filming *The Last Song* in Tybee Island in Savannah, Georgia that they decided to date. They were pretty isolated while filming so once the cameras stopped rolling they would hang around together. Liam is the tallest guy that Miley has dated as he's a huge 6ft 4in; he's also Australian and loves surfing, not Miley's usual type at all.

Liam Hemsworth

Miley gushed to *Popstar!* magazine at the time: 'Liam is so much fun to work with! The crazy thing is he's such a huge star in Australia, and so to help introduce him to our side of the world was really cool. I know how that feels because I travel all over the world on tour and I'm more well known here than I am in some of the places I've visited. So I totally know where he's coming from!'

Liam told the same magazine: 'Miley is great! We had a lot of fun, she's always bright and happy and it's a pleasure to work with her. We got along really well and became good friends during the shoot.'

Miley was really sad on the last day of filming the movie because she didn't want it to be the end. She didn't want to have to say goodbye to Liam so she was over the moon when he said he would go to Nashville for a while so they could hang out.

Her parents Billy Ray and Tish were happy that Miley met Liam and thought he was really nice. Miley added: 'My dad's just happy that I have something going on in my life with someone normal. No psychos, so that's good.'

Miley accidentally forgot when their one-year anniversary was when she was on the *Regis and Kelly* show but she knew it had just passed. Normally it's boys who forget anniversaries but we can't blame Miley –

she's had such a hectic year and they did go from being friends to boyfriend and girlfriend gradually.

Poor Liam has to put up with people sometimes not understanding his Australian accent and they think he's saying his name's Leon. Now he and Miley make a joke of it and she calls him Kevin.

She loved him so much when they were dating but there were still things she wanted to change about him. When he asked her what during an unscripted interview she told the people watching at home: 'He has a real problem. Liam. I know is really cute an' all but he has a picking his nose problem. I'll look over and his finger will be literally in his brain, like you'll see his finger popping out like this (pretends to be picking her nose) coz he's so far into his skull and I'll be like "Please don't" and he's like "Everyone does it." I'm like "I don't".' Miley was worried when they were driving in her car and he started picking his nose because he didn't open the window so she thought he must be putting his snot somewhere else. Yuck!

Liam and Miley are not officially dating any more but they are still good friends. They had an on/off relationship so many fans believe he could still turn out to be Miley's long-term love.

DID YOU KNOW?

Miley was intimidated by Liam's height when she first met him. She thought she'd have to get boxes to stand on all the time. She also knew that he was a big star in Australia so she was a bit nervous about acting alongside him in the beginning but once they started she realised that he was just a nice, down-to-earth guy.

LOL

In the summer of 2010 Miley started filming *LOL: Laughing Out Loud* with Demi Moore. Miley plays the main character, Lola, who has to deal with high school and its dramas while dodging her mum Anne (played by Demi Moore) who is newly single. It's a remake of a 2008 French film but with the same director, Lisa Azuelos.

Miley loves filming movies in the summer months because she spends the rest of the year touring and promoting her singles. She likes to be in the same place for a few months, getting to know the cast and the crew and forming a new movie family. Miley becomes so attached to her movie families that she finds it difficult when they all have to go their separate ways at the end.

Before they started shooting *LOL* Miley was

counting down the days because she was so excited. It was like nothing she'd ever done before and she was looking forward to doing an independent movie without a studio attached. They could just concentrate on making a great movie without the added pressures that having a big studio involved brings. That said she still wants to do more Disney movies in the future because she thinks they are the best movies.

Miley and Demi had great fun shooting the movie but Demi always knew they would because Miley is so grounded and easy to get along with. She also liked having the opportunity to meet the whole Cyrus family. Demi told MTV: 'Miley is a true professional, and she truly has a wonderful family…it really shows'.

Los Angeles

Miley might live in Los Angeles but Tennessee will always be the place where she feels most at home and able to just relax and be herself. She thinks Los Angeles has a totally different vibe and that the people are less trustworthy.

Miley disclosed to the *Daily Mail*: 'It's harder finding people who are real – you don't know what's real and what's fake in this city because almost everyone has a motive and everyone wants to get something.

'So many tell me they are here for new show castings and they'll have their hair and make-up done, ready to be cast – yet they're just nine or ten years old. My sister Noah is nine and she's one of those girls. She'll come home and say: "Oh, I don't think the casting director thought I was pretty," which is heartbreaking.'

Miley has also had to deal with people saying she is too big and that she needs to lose weight to fit into a certain dress. She is absolutely tiny but she's made to feel like she's overweight. This can be really damaging and for a while Miley had days when she just ate one Pop Tart. That was a foolish thing to do – they are supposed to be something people heat up in the toaster for breakfast, not something to be eaten as the only food of the day. Thankfully Miley saw sense and started eating regular meals. She just wants to be healthy now and won't be counting the calories.

Lucas Till

Lucas Till is the actor who played Miley's love interest Travis Brody in *Hannah Montana: The Movie*. Lucas was a bit nervous when he first arrived on set because everyone else had been in the *Hannah Montana* TV

Opposite: Miley creates her very own milkshake at a shop in Los Angeles

Lucas Till

shows so they all knew each other. He soon realised that he had nothing to worry about because Miley soon became his best pal on set and they started hanging out a lot.

When *Seventeen* magazine asked him what it was like to work with Miley he replied, 'So much fun, because you are constantly entertained, whether she means to entertain you or not. You're laughing and having a good time all the time. She's a really sweet girl, and not bad to look at either.

'Sometimes on set, she would ask to pop my knuckles. It hurt! But she'd be like, "Oh, don't be a wuss. Just relax." I cracked her back this morning. I felt a couple of vertebrae realign. Emily Osment has "osteo–old–woman-itis." She can't lift weights or do any physical activity but ride her bike and do yoga. She still cracks her knuckles, though. She taught Miley how to pop her knuckles in weird ways.'

M is for...

Make-up

Miley has been wearing make-up for many years. When she was under the set lights filming *Hannah Montana* she had to wear a lot of make-up otherwise she'd have looked washed out. Even her dad and the male cast members had to wear make-up, whether they wanted to or not.

Because she's spent years with make-up plastered on her face every day Miley likes to go for the natural look when she's on her days off. She hates the way make-up makes her feel, like she's wearing a mask or something. She likes her face just the way it is so will just have chapstick in her handbag for when her lips get dry.

Mandy Jiroux

Mandy Jiroux is one of Miley's best friends. She's five years older than Miley but that doesn't really affect their friendship. Mandy has been one of Miley's *Hannah Montana* dancers for many years, but it wasn't until Miley's best friend Vanessa died that the two of them became close. They started posting funny videos on YouTube and before long they were inseparable. Mandy is like a sister to Miley now and they can both rely on the other for help.

Mandy has become a kind of celebrity herself because of 'The Miley and Mandy Show' videos on YouTube have been viewed by millions of people. Miley and Mandy love going shopping, having sleepovers and filming their show. When they can they film videos together every other day.

Mandy has been dancing forever but being Miley's best friend has made her love singing too. She is a member of a girl group called The Beach Girl5. Like Miley, she also loves dogs and can't wait to get her own one day.

They have matching bracelets that read 'Life's

Good' – and they even gave one to one of the paparazzi.

Michael Poryes

Michael Poryes is a man Miley owes her superstar status to as he is the one of the creators and executive producers of *Hannah Montana*. Prior to *Hannah Montana* Michael had created *That's So Raven*, which was a huge hit for Disney and ran for 100 episodes. Michael worked with two-time Emmy Award winner Steven Peterman to create *Hannah Montana*.

The original idea for *Hannah Montana* came from an episode of *That's So Raven* called 'Goin' Hollywood'. In the episode a child star with a show named after her decides that she wants to go to a normal school. Michael decided to develop the concept and went to Disney with an idea about a teenage rock star who wants to go to school without anyone knowing that she's famous. Disney were impressed and called in Steve Peterman and his writing partner Gary Dontzig. They helped develop the ideas that Michael had come up with and together they made the *Hannah Montana* shows we see on our TV screens.

OPPOSITE: MILEY WITH MANDY JIROUX

Everyone involved in the show loved the overall message it projected – that it's fun to be a celebrity but your family and friends are much more important. Miley herself might be a millionaire but the thing that she cares most about is her family's happiness.

Michael was excited when he started writing the *Hannah Montana* scripts because his son was only ten at the time and he would pitch in, give his thoughts on the script and hang out on set. It was the first time he'd been able to get involved in his dad's work as Michael had been doing shows for adults for a while. Michael liked showing his son bits of the script and watching him start to laugh. In many ways he was the tester – if he found stuff funny then other kids would find it funny too.

Steve Peterman's son was just as involved in the early days of *Hannah Montana*. He would volunteer to help the pizza guys give out free pizzas to the audience on a Friday or do any other odd jobs that needed doing.

In the *Hannah Montana* writers' room (where the writers sit together to come up with story ideas and the direction the show should go in) Michael wanted to have a real mixture of different people. He had someone who was good at story, someone who was good at jokes, someone who was good at sitting back

OPPOSITE: MILEY ON STAGE AS HANNAH MONTANA

and saying when something was wrong or missing. All the writers on *Hannah Montana* had to get along because they spent so much time together cooped up in the writers' room. They all needed to be passionate about the show and what the show was trying to achieve. Small adjustments were made: one writer was replaced the first year, one writer was replaced the second year and two writers were replaced in the third year. Sometimes new writers had to be brought in because the needs of the show had changed.

Originally Michael envisaged Hannah having a mum, a dad, an older brother and a younger brother. They changed their minds and had Hannah with only a dad because they didn't have enough money to pay for all the actors needed for all those characters. They had to choose – would a mum or a dad be better for the storylines? It would have cost $10,000 to have a mum in the pilot and they simply didn't have the cash to spend.

Michael told the audience at a writing masterclass: 'Billy is the secret weapon of the show because he does not have sitcom rhythm to save his life. He is laid back and he takes the whole show when he's in it, and gives it a feel and a texture that we would never have given it because that's not how sitcom writers think. Billy walks quickly to the door; you can write it but he's going to mosey to the door.'

Michael thinks that the *Hannah Montana* phenomena isn't only down to Miley, Billy, the writers or the filming... he thinks everything has had its part to play in the success of *Hannah Montana*.

DID YOU KNOW?

The show wasn't originally going to be called *Hannah Montana*. They came up with a whole host of other names for Miley's rock star alter ego including Anna Cabana, Samantha York and Alexis Texas. Those names seem weird now as no one can imagine any name other than Hannah Montana as the lead character and show title.

Mistakes

Miley is just a normal girl and she makes mistakes sometimes. She always accepts when she's made mistakes and learns from them. She admitted to the *Daily Telegraph*: 'Every career thing I do can't be perfect and sometimes my decisions are wrong. I always say the minute I stop making mistakes is the minute I stop learning and I've definitely learned a lot.

'When you're a pop star or whatever you always have "people". You always hear, "my people will call your people", but you can't let your people talk for you all the time because you're the only person who knows yourself and what you truly want.'

Thankfully Miley has a great family and friendship network that she can rely on to be totally honest and frank with her. They will let her know when she's made mistakes and help her grow as a person.

Her dad thinks he's the best at making mistakes and he's always telling Miley to do the opposite of what he does. He wants her to learn from his mistakes so that she doesn't have to repeat them herself. Billy Ray told *Sunrise*: 'I play music by ear and I play life by ear.'

Mitchel Musso

Mitchel plays Oliver Oken in *Hannah Montana*. He lives in Texas with his parents when he's not in LA. As well as being an actor Mitchel is a singer and released his first album in June 2009.

He's so glad he was cast as Oliver because it allowed him to meet Miley and they have become really close friends. They talk on the phone all time and they can always rely on each other. He wouldn't mind if Miley called him at 3am because he cares for her so much.

Mitchel has a dog called Stitch who he says is his best friend. All of Miley's closest friends seem to love dogs – it's a good job because she has so many. If she had a

MILEY WITH MITCHEL MUSSO

friend who was scared of dogs they wouldn't be able to visit her at home because her pack would be all over them wanting to be stroked and cuddled.

Like Miley, Mitchel had to have a lot of auditions before he was told he had the part. On his fourth audition he had to read with Miley and Emily. The casting people knew then that Mitchel would be the perfect Oliver.

Mitchel and Miley have been so close for so long and when they were younger they did have a bit of a crush on each other for a while, but they are just friends now. They are like brother and sister.

Mitchel is very similar in personality to Miley and he didn't want to be known as another Disney kid who sings. He writes his own music, has dyed black hair and wears low-slung jeans. When he's on stage he looks nothing like Oliver. He has tattoos, too. Miley might only have one tattoo but Mitchel has two (that we know about). He has 'M M M' on his right wrist which stands for Mason, Mitchel and Marc (Mason and Marc are his brothers). His other tattoo is for his dad and it's on his left shoulder. That one reads 'Sam M Unsurpassed'.

'I probably got my first one when I was 15 or 16,' Mitchel revealed to the *Chicago Tribune*. 'My Dad loved it. My Mom was a little distraught. I've always been the rebellious kid in my family, but they love me – I hope.'

Mitchel isn't afraid to disagree with Miley over who she dates because he cares for, but he refuses to discuss it with the media. He just says he wants Miley to date someone her own age. It's not known if he liked Liam Hemsworth when Miley was dating him. He was three years older than her, though.

If you would like to date Mitchel you might like to know what he finds attractive in a girl. He told IML: I don't like girls who are shy and I get a lot of random girls, like when I go to the mall, none of them want to come up to me, like are they scared of me! They're all bug eyed. I'm not looking for anything more than any other guy. I like a good smile. Pretty eyes. She has to be active, like not play-sports active, but she'll play air hockey, do some pool, go for rides on the Santa Monica Pier. I would much rather have fun with her than do the cool thing.'

Money

Everyone in the media seems to be obsessed with the amount of money Miley makes but she isn't bothered by her vast fortune. She would still act and sing even if she wasn't getting paid – because she loves it so much.

MILEY ON A
SHOPPING TRIP
IN CALIFORNIA

She knows that her money is a blessing so she uses it wisely and to help as many people as she can.

Miley expressed this during an interview with *Glamour* magazine: 'In this industry there are so many things that can take over your life: money, alcohol, drugs – even fashion. People hand you things, and you start to believe life is easy. And it's not like that – you're not supposed to be the person you play in the movies. I'm doing fine, and I'll be able to live comfortably for a while. But I like keeping my mind as far away from money and the material aspects of my job as possible.

'I do have limits on my money. I like calling my mom to ask, "Can I have that?" Because I know I can be spending my money more wisely.'

It's great that Miley is careful with her money and doesn't spend thousands every time she goes out shopping. She knows that money can disappear in an instant so she isn't going to let it rule her life.

Mum

Miley's mum is called Leticia Cyrus (née Finley) but everyone calls her Tish. She married Billy Ray a month after she gave birth to Miley, their first child together. Tish already had two small children, Trace and Brandi, from a previous relationship but Billy Ray was the one who adopted them when they were small and brought them up. After Miley they had two more children, Braison and Noah.

Miley and her mum are super close and she goes to work with Miley every day to make sure that she's happy and safe. She has always insisted that Miley maintains as normal a teenage life as possible and won't let her work too hard. When Nick Jonas and Miley broke up it was Tish who supported Miley through it.

Tish is Miley's rock and she's always there for Miley when she needs help or advice. Her love for cheerleading was what got Miley into cheerleading in the first place, and gave her the inner confidence to go for auditions.

Tish did so well raising Miley and her brothers and sisters when Billy Ray was on the road and couldn't be with her. She's a real inspiration to Miley. Sometimes she can be a bit annoying, though, like any mum. She grounds Miley when she misbehaves and takes away some of her things, as Miley explained to tribute.ca: 'My mom can be pretty strict some times. I do get grounded, all the time! She took away my phone, my computer privileges, TV (although I don't watch a lot of TV so that one was OK), but mostly the computer and the phone are the first to go!'

Her mum grounds her when she has tantrums because

she doesn't know what to wear. Because she's always under pressure to look good Miley sometimes needs help but her mum can't understand how she can struggle to put an outfit together when she loves shopping so much. One time Miley got in trouble for saying her mum's cardigan was horrible and looked like it belonged to an old man.

Miley and her mum are so close that sometimes they fight like cat and dog but they always make up. They are like sisters rather than mother and daughter, really. When Miley was fourteen they would go out and children would think that her mum was Hannah Montana because she has long blonde hair whereas Miley has brown hair in real life.

Having a great mum has made Miley want to have her own kids in the next ten years. She wants to go to football matches in silly heels and support her kids – although she hasn't revealed exactly how many kids she would like.

One of the things that Miley is always conscious of is the need to make her parents proud of her. 'The last thing I ever want to do is disappoint my parents. My mom's dad died when she was eighteen, and if something ever happened to one of my parents, I'd want them to go knowing I made them proud,' Miley told *Glamour*, 'I think it's selfish to go out partying all the time, especially if you have little ones [in your family]. I have a nine-year-old sister, and I don't want her to go to school and have people make fun of her for it.'

As well is being close to her mum Miley is extremely close to her grandma too. She thinks she is a lot like her grandma as she is very loyal. When Miley goes out and she's not wearing much make-up her grandma will tell her to put some more blusher on. Miley's grandma loves make-up and always has it on. Miley prefers to call her Mammie rather than grandma.

Music

Music is Miley's passion. Ever since she joined her dad onstage when she was four, Miley has always wanted to entertain. She grew up around some music greats and will never forget being on stage with the likes of Aretha Franklin and Dolly Parton.

Miley has always said that music is the love of her life so she must have been over the moon when she was told that she would be bringing out an album. In 2007 the double album *Hannah Montana 2/Meet Miley Cyrus* was released. It was a huge hit as fans rushed out to buy it. It was number one in America, number three in Canada and number nine in the UK.

Above left: Miley out shopping with one of her best friends, Mandy Jiroux.

Above right and below left: Miley wears some incredible outfits when she's on stage, like these from her 2009 tour.

Below right: Miley looking gorgeous at the Jingle Bell Ball in London.

Miley loves dogs – here, she is pictured with her dog Mate and out on a walk with her dad Billy Ray.

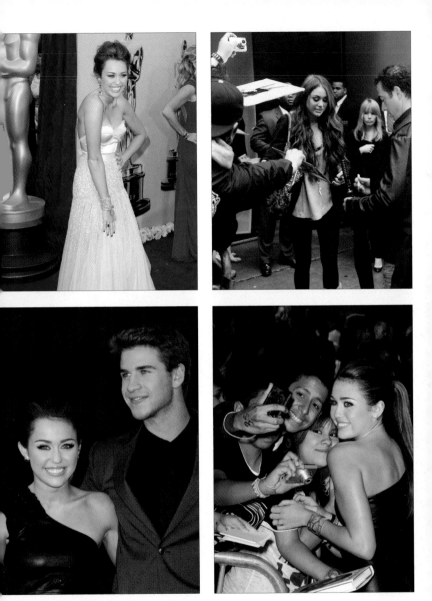

Above left: In March 2010, Miley had the incredible honour of presenting the award for Best Original Song at the Oscars ceremony in Hollywood.

Above right: Miley is mobbed by fans wherever she goes!

Below left and right: Miley looked amazing at the premiere of *The Last Song* – here she is with Liam Hemsworth and chatting to fans at the big event.

Above left: The Cyrus family – Billy Ray, Brandi, Tish, Noah and Trace.

Above right: Miley loves coming to the UK and loves meeting her British fans, as she did at the Radio 1 studios in London in June 2010.

Below: Although Miley isn't that keen on exercise, she does love riding her bike around her California home.

Above: Fans just can't get enough of Miley and she's used to performing in front of thousands of people.

Below left: Miley is always happy to sign autographs.

Below right: Miley performing with one of her heroes, Bret Michaels.

Above left: Miley loves clothes and always looks amazing!

Above right: Miley at the 2010 MuchMusic Video Awards, where she won International Video of the Year for 'Party in the USA'.

Below left and right: Miley and Liam Hemsworth out and about in California.

Above left: Miley's job takes her all over the world – she's pictured here at the airport returning from filming *LOL* in Detroit.

Above right: Miley didn't find learning to drive very easy, but she got her driving licence in the end!

Below left: Miley with Tish and Noah.

Below right: Miley in yet another amazing dress at the 2010 MTV Europe Music Awards.

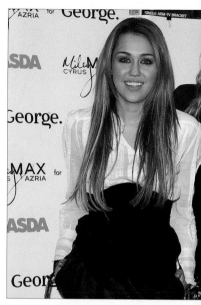

Miley has a much more grown-up look now that she's not playing Hannah Montana. It can't be easy growing up in the spotlight but Miley doesn't let it get her down – she works hard and is sure to be a huge star for many years to come.

Miley was most proud of the ten songs on the *Meet Miley Cyrus* disc as she explained to Wal-Mart Soundcheck: 'My Miley album is a little different from Hannah Montana because I wrote a lot of the songs on the album and I think that makes it more personal, and the title of the album is *Meet Miley Cyrus* and that's exactly what this album is. It's meeting me and introducing myself and what I've gone through more than just the *Hannah Montana* thing.

'My *Meet Miley Cyrus* stuff is kind of rock'n'roll and then its also got a little bit of a pop vibe which is kind of, it's very meeting me, meeting my style. I mean some things are more techno, and some things have lots of guitar, it's so weird like you've kind of got to listen to the music to understand. There's no way to give it a certain style.'

Miley's second studio album *Breakout* came out in July 2008 and it managed to perform even better – it was the number 1 album in the America, Canada and Australia. It charted at number 10 in the UK.

Her third studio album was called *Can't Be Tamed* and came out in June 2010. It was very different from her first two studio albums. The album presents a new, grown-up Miley and isn't about Hannah Montana at all. Miley was given more control over the music and she was able to show her true personality. She was able to make the album exactly how she wanted it to be, which she hadn't had as much freedom to do with her earlier albums.

As well as her three studio albums, Miley has released two live albums: *Hannah Montana & Miley Cyrus: Best of Both Worlds Concert* and the EP *iTunes Live from London* (only available for download). She also released *The Time of Our Lives* album to promote her clothing line. And she has appeared on soundtrack albums *Hannah Montana: The Movie*, *Bolt* and *The Last Song: Original Soundtrack*. On 19 October 2010 a new soundtrack from *Hannah Montana* was released. It was called *Hannah Montana Forever* and contained eleven tracks. The sixth track 'Need a Little Love', featured Sheryl Crow.

Miley likes listening to music whenever she can; it's her favourite thing to do when she's got a spare five minutes, so when she's travelling by plane or tour bus she can usually be seen with her headphones on. She can just lay back, close her eyes and let the music sooth and relax her. Miley is a big fan of The Beatles and John Lennon. Her favourite two tracks are 'Imagine' and 'Jealous Guy'.

If Miley wasn't acting or singing she wouldn't mind as long as she could still be a songwriter. She's been writing songs since she was seven and never wants to stop. She

MILEY WITH SHERYL CROW

gets so much pleasure from writing her own songs about what she's experienced in her life. She's got a shelf full of journals with her songs in – she's written well over a hundred.

N is for...

Names

Miley was given the name Destiny Hope when she was born because her parents thought she was destined for great things. When she was a baby she was always smiling so they soon stopped called her Destiny and started calling her Smiley. Just before she started at school her mum said it would be better if they called her Miley rather than Smiley so she wouldn't be picked on for having Smiley as her name. Billy Ray agreed and she's been Miley ever since. Only Mammie (her grandma) calls her Destiny Hope now.

In January 2008 Miley legally changed her name to

Miley shows how she got her name, 'Smiley'!

Miley Ray Cyrus. She wanted to be legally Miley, and picked Ray as her middle name in memory of her Pappy (her grandad).

Miley might have an unusual name but in the last few years quite a few people have been naming their baby girls Miley. As Miley explained to the *Sun*, this is a bit annoying: 'In a lot of ways it is an honour for your name to be put into all those kinds of things, but then again it's kind of sad. I like being one of the only ones. I have just moved into a new neighbourhood and the girl just three doors down from me is called Miley too. It's spelt differently though. I was so disappointed.'

Miley has learnt to answer to the name Hannah Montana when she's out and about because that's who lots of her young fans think she is – and not just an actress playing a part. Originally the *Hannah Montana* writers planned for Miley Stewart to be called Zoe Stewart, and then Chloe Stewart, but they changed their minds once they cast Miley.

Miley's dad calls her Bud and Little Bud in real life and the producers noticed and decided that Miley on *Hannah Montana* should be called Bud by her dad too.

Noah Cyrus

Noah

Noah is Miley's youngest sister. She's seven years younger than Miley and is the youngest Cyrus child. She loves cheerleading and acting, and many people see her as a mini Miley. Miley might be the eldest but her little sis is the clever one – she uses words Miley doesn't even understand!

Because Noah is young, Miley's parents want to protect her for as long as possible so they don't have thousands of channels on the TVs in their house, only ten. Miley says they miss out on all the gossip shows and don't really buy gossip-type magazines either. They generally miss out on the negative news stories about Miley too because they don't look out for it, and concentrate on having fun as a family instead.

O is for...

Oscars

Miley was given the great honour of presenting at the 2010 Oscars. She presented the Best Original Song Oscar with *Mamma Mia!* star Amanda Seyfried. Both Miley and Amanda looked stunning in their long gowns, although Miley looked at bit nervous as she presented the award, but who can blame her – there were 41 million people watching her on TV!

Earlier that day while Miley was getting pampered and styled, she was photographed for charity. The money raised went to the people of Haiti.

After the awards finished she went to Elton John's

MILEY AND TISH AT
THE 2010 OSCARS

Oscar Party with Liam Hemsworth. It's regarded as the best party to go to and is held at the Pacific Design Center in West Hollywood. Miley was surrounded by some of the biggest stars in Hollywood: Nicole Richie, will.i.am, Jennifer Hudson, Jonas Brothers and Demi Lovato all had a great night.

The year before Miley had been invited to the same party but she'd decided to go home with her mum instead so they could hang out in their PJs. She only goes to big celebrity parties when she really wants to.

P

is for...

Paparazzi

One of the worst things about being famous is being followed by the paparazzi every day. Poor Miley can't go anywhere without groups of men running after her demanding she look at them so they can get a good shot. They hound her when she's driving too, so she's had some scary experiences in the past year. Miley actually pictures them as being those girls who bullied her at school; she doesn't let them bully her into staying inside so she can avoid them because she's not going to be intimidated. She just tries to ignore them and carries on doing things that normal teenagers do.

MILEY IS PHOTOGRAPHED WHEREVER SHE GOES

Billy Ray vented his frustration when being interviewed by *Access Hollywood*: 'You know, when I see people taking pictures of my little girl, I usually try to get them [his driver] to roll down the window to get a picture of them because I just wanna know who's stalking my family.'

Miley spoke of how she felt about the paparazzi sometimes: 'The other day I felt a little bit in danger for the first time because there were too many photographers following me in too many cars. And I have to ask myself, "Why would any other 50-year-old man who was stalking a 17-year-old girl go to jail, but not these guys? I'm not as American as anyone else?"' Miley confided in *Parade* magazine. 'I mean, they couldn't sit outside of a high school but they can sit outside my recording studio. It's creepy.'

Miley isn't afraid to tell her fans what the paparazzi are really like. She can't really have a go at them face to face because they would just ignore her and take photos of her looking angry to sell to magazines. She wrote on her blog: 'Honestly I am so over these photographers! I went to the salon to visit my buddy Scott and bring him a snack and it turned in to total chaos! After I saw him I went with his best friend Fisher to a store he works at and when I was leaving there was at least 30 photographers. It's really scary for me, especially being a new driver! Sorry I'm venting but somehow I feel like my fans are the only people I can talk to. I love you guys, I really miss Nashville today…'

Pappy

Pappy was Miley's grandad – her dad's dad – and he was the person she was closest to before he died. She was devastated when he died in 2006 and she misses him every single day. She has set up The Pappy Cyrus Foundation in his memory, to raise money for children who need help in the US.

She talked to *MediaBlvd Magazine* about how she felt in April 2009: 'This is the third year since my grandad died. That was a hard day because he was like my best friend, so I have a foundation called The Pappy Cyrus Foundation. We're working with all kinds of different people. We actually did a couple of trips back and forth to the White House. One of the reasons I was at the inauguration was so that we could get all of American involved. It's something that's so important. We deal with homeless shelters.

'When I was on tour in 2007, my best friend died of cystic fibrosis, right after my granddad had died, so I just had a hard time with cancers and that kind of stuff. That's mostly who I work with. Then, I did a tour with

The Jonas Brothers and we ended up raising $2.5 million for City of Hope, which went to cures and studies for kids. It was really amazing to watch the process. We got to go to the hospitals and watch them do all these crazy things. We were sitting there watching live cells being placed and it was amazing. That was one of the coolest experiences.'

Miley will never forget Pappy and the lessons that he taught her. He inspired her so much. Visiting him when she knew he was dying was really hard and she wrote the song 'I Miss You' for him just before he died.

Parents

Miley's parents always provided a loving home for her and her siblings. But sometimes things just don't work out, and on 26 October 2010 Billy Ray filed for divorce from Miley's mum Tish, citing 'irreconcilable differences'. They released a joint statement the next day to US magazine *People*. They said: 'As you can imagine, this is a very difficult time for our family. We are trying to work through some personal matters. We appreciate your thoughts and prayers.'

Party in the USA

'Party in the USA' was a track that Miley released in 2009. It was a surprise hit for Miley because she'd released it to promote her clothing line. Miley was asked by Wal-Mart to help design a clothing line that reflected her own style, was affordable, and fitted real girls and women. Miley loved the jeans from her collection and wore them every day for a while; she liked the way they fitted perfectly and how good she felt in them.

The song wasn't one that Miley would have naturally chosen but people everywhere fell in love with it and it ended up reaching number 1 in the US, number 3 in Canada and New Zealand and number in Japan. It reached number 11 in the UK.

Even though it did brilliantly, Miley's other songs are more special to her because she actually wrote them. 'Party in the USA' was written by Lukasz Gottwald, Claude Kelly and Jessica Cornish, so Miley didn't have a part to play in the lyrics. She might sing about Jay-Z on the track, but when she first picked the song she had never heard a Jay-Z track.

Peter Chelsom

Blackpool-born Peter Chelsom was the director of *Hannah Montana: The Movie*. He is a very experienced director, actor and producer but hasn't always made commercially successful films. Many people thought he was a weird choice for the Hannah Montana film but he did a great job. He has worked with big stars before: John Cusack and Kate Beckinsale in *Serendipity* and Richard Gere and Jennifer Lopez in *Shall We Dance*.

Peter might have directed some great actors in the past but when he watched Miley on *Oprah* he was blown away. He thought she was incredibly talented and should be up there with Shirley Temple, Judy Garland and Barbra Streisand. He thinks she is such an awesome performer and that she shows so much potential because she has so much talent for someone still only in her teens.

Peter had been quite nervous about the kissing scene in *Hannah Montana: The Movie* because of the fuss Miley's *Vanity Fair* photo shoot had caused just a few weeks before. He told the *Telegraph*: 'I never wanted tongues. Absolutely no swapping of saliva. Miley is a role model for nine-year-olds. I don't want to upset them or their mothers.'

Miley likes to look her best when she's filming her movies or TV shows, but Peter wanted to capture the real Miley on-screen so he banned her from getting her make-up retouched when she was sweating, and from wearing her hair extensions. He wanted her hair to look messy, and he didn't want her to look too brown from spray tans, either. It must have been quite difficult for Miley to just go with the flow and forget about how she looked.

Peter enjoyed working with Taylor Swift too, even though she was only on set for one day. He told E! Online: 'I've made a very big mental check to work with her again.

If she walked in the room right now, I would say: "Can we meet and talk about films you might want to do?" I don't have anything concrete, but I would be very keen to do something with her.'

Hannah Montana: The Movie was such a big hit that it took $34 million in the first weekend and Peter got a lot more calls about possible projects he might want to do in the future. In many ways he has Miley to thank for reviving his career as she is the main reason kids rushed out to see the movie.

Photo shoots

Miley has done hundreds of photo shoots for various magazines and newspapers in the past few years – many fans rush out to buy the magazines as soon as they come out in the shops.

Miley wants all her fans to realise that the Miley Cyrus they see in magazines isn't the real Miley Cyrus. The photos are altered to make Miley look like she has flawless skin with no imperfections. Even before the photos are taken people spend hours doing Miley's hair and make-up and styling her.

Miley announced on *Good Morning America*: 'I wish I could tell every little girl who looks in the mirror and says, "I'm not beautiful", and take them into the process to [see] what it takes to look like that. They would feel so much better about themselves. It takes an hour and a half before you're even there and they're [already] working on the lighting... it's not real.'

Miley doesn't like the way people obsess about the way she looks. She doesn't like the way young Hollywood stars are super skinny either as she explained to *Glamour* magazine in an interview: 'I've been at photo shoots where I've tried something on and said, "Oh my gosh, why don't these fit?" But I'll never be a six-foot-tall, 95-pound model; I'm meant to have a little more meat on my bones. One thing that bugs me is people who say, "Miley really needs to lose some weight," or "She got her boobs done." I did start out really skinny, but you're not going to have boobs when you're twelve

years old. I'm like, what are you talking about – let me grow!'

Piano lessons

When Miley was growing up and went to visit her Pappy in his log cabin she would mess around on his piano, but she never took lessons – she just liked making up her own tunes. When Miley was cast in *The Last Song* she knew that she would have to have piano lessons. Her character Ronnie and Greg Kinnear's character Steve were supposed to be gifted piano players.

Miley impressed everyone with how quickly she mastered the piano after only a couple of lessons. 'Maybe it was easier because I already play guitar. I learned not just how to play a song but how to play it like a classically trained musician, the way to sit, the way you look when you're at the piano, the posture, the fingering,' she said. It's a lot more discipline than just casual playing. The learning experiences are a part of my job I really love. So many people dream of learning something like this and I'm getting this experience along with making a movie.'

OPPOSITE: MILEY ALWAYS LOOKS GORGEOUS IN PHOTO SHOOTS OR ON THE RED CARPET

Plays

Everyone has parts in their school plays and Miley was no different. She never played the main part but she always stood out. She was also in plays when she went to a summer acting camp aged six.

Miley likes to go and see plays on Broadway with her mum and Noah when she can. Some people think it's only a matter of time before she's cast in a big production on Broadway. Lots of famous actors and actresses do a stint on Broadway between movies, or simply to try something new: Katie Holmes, Daniel Radcliffe and Kevin Spacey are just some of the big stars who have graced Broadway.

If Miley wanted to be in a musical or play somewhere else she could perform in London's West End. Nick Jonas made his West End debut in *Les Misérables* in June 2010 and it's rumoured that Kristen Stewart might be considering treading the boards once she's finished playing Bella in the *Twilight* movies. Miley would be a great addition to any cast as she can both sing and act.

Premieres

Miley's first premiere experience was the *Chicken Little* premiere in October 2005. She really wanted to see the film so she managed to get tickets for her and her mum to go. If you try to find a photo of Miley at the premiere you won't have much luck. No one knew who she was so the photographers didn't bother asking her to pose for photos on the red carpet. It was a bit of a disappointing night for Miley because she expected so much.

Now she can go to any premiere and she is the star attraction. She loves getting the opportunity to meet new people and chat to fans. Miley loves getting ready for premieres and likes to share how she is feeling with her fans. Before her *Hannah Montana: The Movie* premiere she tweeted: 'Getting ready for the red carpet! This is my VERY 1st film I can't believe it's finally here! Thank u! & mommy thank U 4 allowing me 2 dream!'

She must have been disappointed when she couldn't go to the UK premiere for *The Last Song* in April 2010 because of the volcanic ash clouds from Iceland, which meant there were no flights in or out of the UK at the time.

Q is for...

Queen Elizabeth

For many performers getting invited to perform at the Royal Variety Performance is the biggest honour of their lives. Stars love the opportunity to perform for the Queen and to share the stage with some of the most talented acts in the world. Miley was given the special job of opening the 2009 show with a performance of 'Party in the USA'. She was really excited and told people she wanted to teach the Queen the Hoedown Throwdown.

Afterwards she waited in line with the other performers to meet the Queen. She was thrilled to meet Lady Gaga too – it was an awesome night for her Blackpool.

R is for...

Relaxing

If Miley wants to relax she won't go to a spa to have a massage. Having to lie down and keep quiet for an hour while someone massages her just doesn't appeal. She loves to talk so much that it would be impossible for her to stay silent.

When Miley wants to relax she likes to lie on her bed and listen to music, or take her dogs for a walk. She also likes playing her guitar. Music soothes her and allows her to escape from the stresses of being a celebrity.

Whenever things get too much she can talk to her

mum or read her Bible; she knows she doesn't have to go through it alone.

Ronnie

Ronnie is the name of Miley's character in *The Last Song*. Nicholas Sparks wrote both the script and the novel, and he asked Miley to come up with the name of the lead character. She could have picked any name in the world but she picked Ronnie because her pappy was called Ron, and they adapted it to Ronnie. Ron wouldn't have quite worked as a girl's name!

Nicholas actually wrote *The Last Song* with Miley in mind. He's been contacted by the producer Jennifer Gibgot who wanted to know if he had a script that would suit Miley and show off her acting skills. He didn't have anything so he set about writing something, and six weeks later he had developed *The Last Song*.

Nicholas insists: 'The finished product is definitely not a *Hannah Montana* movie. It's an ensemble piece with a talented cast that will appeal to audiences of all ages. Ronnie is a really compelling female character going through things that a lot of teenagers are going through. She's forced to really grow and mature through the course the film.'

Miley thinks there are lots similarities between her

and Ronnie. 'Mostly through the love of music. Mostly what she learns later is all about love and forgiveness and second chances – you know, in the career I'm in I have to do that a lot.

'There's no room for grudges and bitterness. She learns that later it's all about love and the people around you. And I think it's really beautifully done the way she has that transition and learns,' she told MTV.

Rumours

Some people enjoy spreading rumours about Miley. They don't care whether it upsets Miley, her family, her friends or her fans. They just want to see people react and enjoy making things up.

In November 2008 hackers used Miley's personal YouTube account to post a video saying that she'd died. They said she'd been run over by a drunk driver. Scared fans believed what the video said because they thought that Miley's best friend Mandy had posted it. As soon as the real Mandy found out she posted a message on her official MySpace to say Miley was perfectly fine and that someone had hacked into their account.

The internet allows rumours to be spread in a matter of seconds, so a lot of fans would have seen the video before it was taken down. It's horrible that people can enjoy upsetting others by posting such lies.

S is for...

School

Miley is so nice that it's hard to believe that she was bullied at school. She hated having to go every day because she was picked on constantly by girls who pretended to be her friends.

At school she enjoyed learning other languages but she hated maths.

Once she started filming *Hannah Montana* she got the chance to leave school and she was so happy. She would never have to see those bullies ever again. When they were filming the show she had a special tutor and in the breaks in between she went to a special school called

Options For Youth. The students here either have a one-to-one tutor or are in a small group and share a tutor. Lots of people thought that Miley's tutor would let her off if she forgot to do her homework or performed badly in an exam, but this wasn't the case at all. Miley's tutor always demanded that she worked extra hard because everyone was watching to see how she did.

A journalist from IML (the 'It's My Life' website) asked Miley what her schedule was like at school. She replied: 'It's intense! My shooting schedule is easy compared to what I do at school. This was the rule, that acting and singing is my "side stuff". If you came to my school you'd see a whole different side of me. There I'm like, okay, it's time to get down and study.'

These days, Miley still studies but her teacher tries to keep her distance because Miley started trying to get away when she saw her. She was having so much fun that she didn't want to start learning about geography or history. To combat this Miley's teacher has started handing her assignments, walking away and then returning later in the day to collect the finished assignment. This way Miley gets to take her time and fit the work in when she wants, as long as it's completed by the end of the day. She's still learning but is not dreading it as much as she used to.

Miley is really looking forward to finishing twelfth grade next year, as this is the year when US students graduate (usually at eighteen). Miley will probably take a break from studying because in her mind people go to uni to get a job and she already has a job. In the future she might change her mind and want to challenge herself by gaining a degree, but for now she's just happy singing and acting. She told Q100 Atlanta's Bert Show: 'My sister went to MTSU in Nashville, so I'd probably want to be there with all my friends, but I'm not gonna go to college right now. I am a firm believer that you can go back at any age you want, because my grandma went back to college at 62 years old.'

7 Things

When Miley is going through tough times she likes to write songs. They help focus her mind, and writing a song and singing it allow her an outlet for her emotions. Not all of Miley's songs have been released; some are just personal ones that she can play on her own if she wants.

Miley released '7 Things' on 17 June 2008. It was the first song she released from her album *Breakout*. When her fans listened to the song they instantly thought it was about Nick Jonas because he and Miley had recently broken up after two years together.

Popstar! magazine asked her about the rumours. She said: '[With] "7 Things" I think a lot of people do, you know, think it's about Nick Jonas, and if they think it is, that's fine, or whoever they think it's about. But mostly that song is about who, um, they want it to be to. Like mostly, it's if a girl hates her current, or ex-boyfriend – for me it's an ex-boyfriend – so I think, you know, like, Nick is someone that was really important in my life, but I don't hate him. It's a good song and it's fun.'

Miley might have written the song because of Nick but he didn't think it was about him when he heard it because of some of the lyrics. He doesn't think he's insecure at all and he doesn't think his friends are uncool, so he doesn't think the guy the song is aimed is him.

Miley will probably always hate and love Nick but she's just glad she was able to make something positive happen after their horrible breakup. '7 Things' was a big hit right across the world – it appeared in the top ten charts of the US, Japan, Australia and Norway.

Sharks

Miley never wants to let people down and when she found out she would have to spend some time in a shark tank during the filming of *The Last Song* she knew she couldn't back out.

She found being with the sharks at the Georgia Aquarium scary but at least she had Liam with her. He had never scuba-dived before so they both had a lot of learning to do before the cameras could start rolling.

Some of the aquarium workers told Miley before her scene that the sharks would be hungry as they hadn't fed them for a few days. This was to make sure that they swam close to Miley and Liam (thinking they were going to get fed). This must have panicked Miley but there was no need for her to be alarmed as sharks can go many days in the wild without feeding. Miley made sure that people took photos of her with the sharks so she could keep them as mementos of that amazing day.

Sleep

Miley is so busy that she rarely has time to have a lie-in. Sometimes she would like nothing better than to crawl under the covers and have a few extra hours sleep, but she can't. Her schedule is so packed that if she got up late she'd miss filming or being interviewed. If it was down to her she'd get up at 12.30 each day. Once she stayed in bed until 4pm on a day off and her mum came in to check if she was still alive.

Miley now understands what it's like for famous people. We might think that they have an easy life doing fun stuff but they actually work really long hours. Miley told a journalist from *Harpers Bazaar*: 'I remember so many times when I was younger being like, "Why does Dad sleep so much when he's home from the road?", "Why doesn't Dad want to play?" Now I'm starting to get it. When I come home from the road, the first thing I do is grab my baby sister [Noah] and hold her for as long as she'll let me.'

Sometimes Miley has real problems getting a good night's sleep because she can't stop waking up in the night. She tweeted: 'insomnia – difficulty in falling or staying asleep, sleeplessness. i have just diagnosed myself. i am an insomniac.

'Why do i wake up at 5am everyday... i just wanna sleep until my alarm goes off!!! is that so much to ask! :([sic].'

When Miley wakes up she finds herself thinking a lot about different things in her life and that makes her even more tired. She just wants to be able to shut her eyes and dream without having to think about stuff she has to do the next day. On other occasions, songs that she has been listening to in the daytime pop into her head and stop her

OPPOSITE: MILEY PERFORMS IN NEW YORK DESPITE NOT HAVING HAD MUCH SLEEP!

drifting off to sleep. She recently couldn't get Lady Gaga's 'Poker Face' out of her head, however hard she tried.

On 25 July 2008 Miley performed a free concert in New York even though she'd only had one and a half hours' sleep. She'd been so nervous that she couldn't sleep, but once she saw her fans she knew she would be okay and that she was ready to rock the place.

Lots of kids like jumping in their parents' bed when they have nightmares but most grow out of it by the time they are seven or eight. Miley still likes to sleep with her parents (even when she hasn't had a nightmare). She confessed to America's *Glamour* magazine: 'At times I feel I'm very mature for my age, but other times I feel very immature. I still like to sleep with my parents sometimes. I'll go into their bedroom and snuggle with my mum, because I've been working all day and haven't seen her. Or my dad will give me a piggyback ride. I'm not around other people my age that much, so I don't know how sixteen-year-olds are supposed to act! I just do what feels right.'

Sometimes when people get little sleep they can be prone to sore throats and feeling under the weather. Poor Miley had to go into work when she had a sore throat during the filming of *Hannah Montana* season 4. Her voice sounded croaky but because she was filming a scene where Hannah was supposed to be feeling run down it was okay. She just had to grit her teeth and bear it. There were reporters from around the world on set that day doing behind-the-scenes filming so she had to do interviews too.

Smoking

Twilight stars Robert Pattinson and Kristen Stewart might smoke but Miley will never ever try a cigarette. She knows at first hand what smoking can do because one of her grandads who smoked died of lung cancer.

She also knows smoking would be a stupid thing to do because she's a singer and it might damage her voice. She wants to protect herself and tries to not be around people who smoke.

T is for...

Tattoo

Miley has a tattoo just below her heart that reads 'Just Breathe'. She wasn't the first member of the Cyrus family to visit a tattoo parlour. Her mum, dad, sister Brandi and brother Trace all have tattoos.

Miley got the tattoo in memory of her friend Vanessa who had cystic fibrosis and her two grandads who died of lung cancer. She explained why she picked Just Breathe to *Harpers Bazaar*: 'It reminds me not to take things for granted. I mean, breathing – that was something none of them could do, the most basic thing. And I put it near my heart, because that is where they will always be.'

She hates needles but she was determined to get her tattoo. She knew it would hurt but she wanted a permanent reminder of the people she loved. She can touch her tattoo whenever she wants and think about what it means to her. Miley's tattoo is very personal to her and she doesn't feel the need to show it off. In the future she might get another tattoo but she would only if it meant something to her; she wouldn't get one just for the sake of it.

Miley is a bit of a tattoo designer and she was the one who designed the tiny heart on her dad's hand. He was sat in church with Miley and she drew it on him. He'd said that day was Miley day and they could do whatever she wanted. After church she said she wanted him to turn the doodle into a tattoo. She also took him to a hairdresser and had highlights put in his hair!

Taylor Swift

Miley is very close to fellow singer and actress Taylor Swift. They have a lot in common and both used to date a Jonas Brother. If things had worked out they could have ended up as sisters-in-law.

Taylor was thrilled to have a guest appearance in *Hannah Montana: The Movie* because she thinks Miley's great. She announced on the *Today* show that she was

<small>Taylor Swift</small>

also really excited because she wanted to be able to tell her fans that love *Hannah Montana* that she got to be in the movie. They would be so impressed.

It wasn't just Taylor's fans who were glad that she was cast – Miley was too. She told MTV: 'It was pretty pro [on set], because we were all working and stuff, but we had fun. We actually didn't get to hang out that much while we shot because she was in such a quick scene, but it was fun to have her on set. She's cool.'

As well as acting in the movie, Taylor also recorded 'Crazier' for the movie soundtrack. Miley likes Taylor's country-music style but isn't sure that she'd release country tracks herself. She prefers pop.

Teeth

Miley might have teeth that look perfect now but when she was younger she had to wear braces. Child actors and actresses are always put under pressure to look 100 per cent perfect all the time. As soon as she finished filming the *Hannah Montana* pilot they sent her to the dentist.

Poor Miley got teased by her brother for wearing braces and it made her not want to wear them. She ended up getting them removed after four months. Back then she felt very self-conscious but now she realises that her braces didn't make her look stupid after all and that if she'd kept her retainer in she would have even straighter teeth now.

The Last Song

Playing Ronnie in *The Last Song* might have been Miley's biggest challenge to date. She was so busy filming *Hannah Montana* and touring that it was almost impossible to fit it in but she somehow managed it. She thinks it was just meant to be: if she hadn't been in the movie she might have never met Liam Hemsworth and she wouldn't have grown as much as a person as she did in those months she was on Tybee Island filming.

The director, producers and cast all thought Miley did an amazing job, but Miley herself still thinks she needs acting lessons. She said that once she saw the movie she'd book an acting coach. She wants to improve and become a great adult actress.

Miley had decided to record 'When I Look At You' for her album but it ended up being the film's biggest and more memorable song. She told MyParkMag what happened: 'When we realised it describes this entire movie, we had a composer come in and make a piano piece for me to be able to play. It's in the movie when

MILEY AND LIAM HEMSWORTH AT THE PREMIERE OF THE LAST SONG

Ronnie reveals to Will that she plays the piano. It was perfect for that scene because it's a love song, but it's also about God, about family, about love – it's kind of what this movie is all about.'

Miley's mum was the executive producer on the movie so she had a big role to play on set. Miley and her family have their own production company called Cyrus' Hope Town Entertainment, which has a production deal with Disney. Miley isn't the first star to have her own production company. Taylor Lautner has one with his dad, and other big stars like Jennifer Aniston and Tom Cruise have their own too. It helps them to have control over the movies they make.

Miley loved the time she spent in Tybee filming *The Last Song*. She told *Harpers Bazaar*: 'I went out every night with my friends. I did karaoke. I danced. All this stuff would've been such a big deal in Los Angeles: Who's she with? Why is she dancing? I felt alive and real. It's so much easier to know who you are when there aren't a thousand people telling you who they think you are. I felt like I was really figuring myself out. Usually I have someone whispering in my ear, but I was on my own.'

She's even said she enjoying filming *The Last Song* a bit more than filming an episode of *Hannah Montana* because she's been filming *Hannah Montana* for such a long time and it's a different experience filming a movie. She might have enjoyed it more but it was much tougher to do – Ronnie was in many ways a harder character to play than Hannah Montana.

Time

Time has become even more precious to Miley in the last couple of years. She so rarely has any spare time to do her own thing that when she gets the chance she likes to try a new hobby or visit the people she loves the most.

Miley might be like her mum in many ways but not when it comes to time. Her mum gets really stressed when they are running late; Miley is a lot more relaxed and doesn't see the sense in rushing. Also, she can't be like her mum because she has to stay calm due to her heart condition.

One time Miley was having a dream where both her mum and Madonna were yelling at her, telling her to wake up, and then her mum woke her up in real life yelling at her to get up because they were running late. Not surprisingly, Miley found that totally weird.

Miley's time is so precious that sometimes she has to turn down interviews and opportunities she would like to take. She can't work 24/7 or she would make herself ill. She might miss out sometimes, but on the whole she's happy with the way she spends her time.

Miley would love to have kids and a husband to go home to one day. Then she'll realise that when she thought she had no time to herself she actually had loads. She'll have to divide herself between filming, singing and spending time with her husband and kids. She'll probably have to say no to a lot more projects, but knowing Miley, she won't mind.

Touring

Miley is passionate about touring because she gets to meet her fans and she loves being on stage and performing. It makes her feel alive and happy.

You would think she'd hate being stuck in her tour bus but she actually likes travelling and sleeping in it because her mum designed it to be just like their home in California. Plus, Noah, their dogs and a whole host of other members of the Cyrus family travel with her, making it less likely she'll get homesick.

The biggest downside is the food she has to eat on tour because it's nowhere near as good as the food she gets at home. She loves her mum's cooking.

The other thing Miley dislikes about touring is performing the same songs again and again, every night

MILEY ON
STAGE IN SPAIN

in the same order. She would prefer it if things changed each night like they do when she's filming *Hannah Montana* and she gets a new script every day. She doesn't want to just go through the motions. Every night she sets herself the challenge of beating the performance from the night before.

Her brothers and sisters like winding her up on tour – once they used her toothbrush to brush their hair and eyebrows. Yuck! They also have to share one bathroom, which is quite a challenge because there are so many people travelling and the bathroom on the tour bus isn't the biggest.

When the tour bus parks up at a new venue Miley rushes inside and heads for a shower. She can't have hot showers on her tour bus so she doesn't bother: her cheeky brothers always use the hot water up so she has the choice of a cold shower or no shower.

Her dad is probably the only member of her family who hasn't stayed on her tour bus. Miley doesn't seem to mind. He still comes to support her but goes home afterwards to look after her brother and sister and their animals. He's seen her perform in concert quite a few times, and loved every second of seeing his little girl doing what she loves the most.

When one of Miley's fans asked her if she ever gets nervous singing in front of thousands of people she replied, 'Really, now it's like second nature. I know my body is ready to perform at certain times. My mom was laughing the other day when I didn't have a show. At 5 o'clock, when I usually would be warming up, I was super-hyper. She's, like, "You're just so used to being ready to go at 5."'

Miley was criticised in the press when a Hannah Montana double was used during her concert. Her PR company issued the following statement to explain why this happened: 'To help speed the transition from Hannah to Miley, there is a production element during the performance of "We Got the Party" incorporating a body double for Miley.

'After Hannah has completed the featured verse on the duet with the Jonas Brothers, a body double appears approximately one to two minutes prior to the end of the song in order to allow Miley to remove the Hannah wig and costume and transform into Miley for her solo set. Other than during this very brief transitional moment in the show, Miley performs live during the entirety of both the Hannah and Miley segments of the concert.'

Miley was asked about it during an interview with *USA Today* shortly after the reports came out. She said: 'We don't even do it any more because we changed songs. But it wasn't for the reason everyone was saying

MILEY ON
STAGE IN
PORTLAND,
OREGON

– because I'm not singing, because I'm not this, because I'm not that. It was a total technical thing. When I'm shooting *Hannah Montana*, it takes me an hour and a half to go from Hannah to Miley. [Onstage], I have a minute, 50 seconds. There's no way; I need a good three to four minutes. So I did have to take a double to dance for that minute.'

Trace

Trace is Miley's oldest brother and is four years older than her. People might think that Noah is the sibling that Miley is most like but she would disagree. She thinks her personality is most like that of Trace.

Trace and Miley share the same mum, and Billy Ray adopted Trace when he was a small boy. Trace loves music like the rest of the Cyrus family and used to be in a band called Metro Station.

Trace played the lead guitar and met his band mate Mason Musso thanks to Miley and *Hannah Montana*. Mason's brother Michel plays Oliver in the show and it was their mums who suggested they form a band. They broke up in early 2010 and Trace joined another band called Ashland HIGH.

Trace has lots of tattoos and is very rock and roll. He likes it that his parents have always let him

Trace

express himself and have not banned him from getting more tattoos.

Travelling

Miley has clocked up thousands of air miles while promoting her movies, TV shows and music. She is used to being in one country one day and another country the next.

During long flights Miley tries to catch up with sleep and doesn't watch movies like a lot of her fellow passengers do. She might read some chapters of a book or chat to her travel companions.

Miley's big ambition is to travel more and she has a map that she sticks stickers on when she visits a country. She likes looking at the map and knowing that even if she never visits that country again she's been there at least once. She must have a lot of stickers on her map by now.

Twilight

Miley was flattered when she heard that Kristen Stewart listened to her music to get into character for *Twilight*. She isn't the biggest *Twilight* fan in the world; in fact she hasn't seen it. She might have watched

Twilight if she hadn't been on tour when it first came out, or if it hadn't been so popular. She's never been one to want to do the 'in' thing just for the sake of it. Maybe one day she'll buy the DVD and decide that vampires aren't that bad after all.

However, she loves Kristen Stewart. She thinks Kristen is a great actress and loved watching her play Joan Jett in the movie *The Runaways*.

Miley's love of Kristen's work might please *Twilight* fans who were left feeling upset and angry when Miley said in April 2009 that she wasn't a fan of the programme, and that girls fall in love with Edward, not Robert Pattinson. Miley did say after meeting Robert in person at the Teen Choice Awards a few months later that she had completely changed her mind, however.

She tweeted: 'Gave a hug to Rob Pattinson today. Ok girls, I get it now. So cute. Sorry "Robby" about all my bashing in the past :)'.

Tyra Banks

Tyra Banks is a model, actress and TV personality in the US. She's most famous for being the creator and host of *America's Next Top Model*. She played herself in *Hannah Montana: The Movie* and she fought with Miley in a scene set in a women's shoe department. It was a funny scene, with the two of them fighting over some shoes and throwing each other around.

Miley did have an accident during filming, as one of the shoes went flying and hit someone. Miley was so concerned she rushed over and wanted to check they were okay and if they needed anything. The director wanted to carry on but Miley wasn't going to carry on until that person was okay.

Tyra found everyone on the *Hannah Montana: The Movie* set really nice to work with and she fitted right in. There were no diva strops off-camera as all the cast and crew got along. Since then Tyra has defended Miley when she has been criticised in the past. She told the presenters of *The View*: 'I just wish everybody would leave her alone!' Miley has also taught Tyra how to dance, showing her how to do the Hoedown Throwdown.

U is for...

UK

Miley loves visiting the UK. She was thrilled when she heard she would be performing for several nights at the O2 in 2009 because it's such a big venue. She didn't think she was well known enough in the UK but she was wrong – she actually broke the attendance record. Her ten concerts sold out in ten minutes.

Miley likes UK fans because they like her for her music and are less bothered about what's going on in her private life. She enjoyed spending time writing songs while she was in the UK, and recorded in the same studio that Bob Marley and the Beatles

Miley performs in London in 2010

recorded some of their biggest tracks. That really inspired Miley.

When Miley visited the UK for the first time she was put on the top of an open double-decker bus for a press event, even though it was freezing. She was driven around London a few times so she got to see all the sights like Buckingham Palace and Big Ben. Being in London for the first time was extra exciting because her mum was ill so couldn't come with her. As soon as Miley arrived she was whisked to Harrods where she splashed out on a Prada purse – her mum wasn't there to supervise! She loved the purse at the time but only used it once before lending to a friend. She now has no idea where it is. Oops!

Miley has been to Ireland too, where she bought her brother a coat for Christmas, and had a great time visiting a park and feeding the ducks. Miley hasn't been to Scotland yet and her Scottish fans really want to see her perform. They've started a petition on the internet in the hope that she will visit either Edinburgh or Glasgow.

V is for...

Vanessa

Vanessa was a very special girl that Miley met when she was visiting sick children in a Los Angeles hospital. Vanessa was only nine when they met for the first time and Miley felt a connection to her straight away. She wanted to get to know Vanessa properly and invited her to visit her on the set of *Hannah Montana*. Vanessa had cystic fibrosis and was very ill. She couldn't do everything a normal nine-year-old girl could do but she still smiled. They became best friends and Vanessa helped Miley realise how precious life is and that her problems were small compared to those of people who are seriously ill.

Miley was devastated when Vanessa died because she thought she would have many more years with her.

She told the *Daily Mail* in an interview: 'Last year I lost one of my closest friends to cystic fibrosis. She was almost 13 and she passed away while I was on tour so I couldn't go back home when it happened. I kind of went crazy. I couldn't understand why it had happened and I was really upset.

'I was touring with the Jonas Brothers and Nick said I had to pull myself together, and he was right because I was going mad.'

Miley has said that she knows she will meet Vanessa again one day in heaven. She is so glad she got to have three years with her.

Virginity

Miley is very happy to be a virgin and has vowed to remain one until her wedding day. She wears a purity ring on her ring finger which symbolises the promise she has made to herself, her family and God. Miley's parents didn't force her to wear one; she made the decision herself when she was old enough. Her mum picked out the ring and it means so much to Miley.

'I like to think of myself as the girl that no one can get, that no one can keep in their hand. Even at my age, a lot of girls are starting to fall, and I think if [abstaining] is a commitment girls make, that's great,' she admitted to *TV Guide* magazine.

Miley isn't he first member of her family to wear a purity ring: her sister Brandi wears one. Her friends The Jonas Brothers, Hilary Duff, Selena Gomez and Jordin Sparks all wear them (or wore them up until they got married).

W is for...

Wake

In June 2010 it was reported that Miley was being considered for a role in another book adaptation – to play the lead character Janie in a movie based Lisa McMann's paranormal thriller novel *Wake*. It would be a joint venture for Paramount Pictures and MTV Films with *Disturbia* co-writer Christopher Landon writing the screenplay.

Wings

Miley was thrilled when she got the news that she would be playing Laurel in the movie *Wings*. Disney haven't given a release date so far, but it's expected that it will be released autumn 2011 or early 2012. Her mum will be the executive producer.

The movie is based on the bestselling book by American author Aprilynne Pike. She is currently writing the fourth and last book of the series so Miley could end up being in a total of four films if the first one is a big hit. Many people think it will be as big as *Twilight*.

Miley's character is the main character in the series. Laurel is a quiet fifteen-year-old who has been home schooled all her life until she moves to California and has to go to high school. She finds things strange at first but makes good friends with a boy called David. He accepts that she is a bit different from other girls (she's a vegan; sunlight seems to shine through her and she never gets cold).

One day, a bump on Laurel's back sprouts into a giant flower. She doesn't know what is going on and she tries to find out with David's help. All they know is that she was left on her parents' doorstep in a basket when she was three.

Later, when she's on her way home she bumps into

Tamani and feels drawn to him. She discovers she isn't human after all and that they are both faeries. She also learns that she was given to her parents so she would inherit their land, which is important to the faeries as it holds the gate to Avalon. When her parents consider selling up they put the faeries at risk – they need to protect the gate to Avalon and Laurel must help save the secret, protect her family and sort out how she feels for David and Tamani. She needs to find out who she is and where she belongs.

Working Out

Miley isn't a big fan of working out and prefers to dance to keep fit. She does support Liam Hemsworth, though, when he's training in the gym and sneaks her tracks onto his playlist. Liam told People.com: 'She does a lot of dancing – so that's her workout. I couldn't keep up with her dancing because she's super flexible and she's throwing her legs up around her head and stuff like that.'

Miley has her own personal trainer to help her keep fit. In 2007 she started working with Harley Pasternak who has trained Jessica Simpson, Kanye West, Lady Gaga and Katy Perry. He is one of the best in the business.

MILEY WITH HER PERSONAL TRAINER

She also works closely with Jamal Sims, who was her choreographer for the 'Can't Be Tamed' video. She came up with the concept for the video with Jamal and made sure she was fit enough to do all the dance moves.

As well as dancing, Miley walks her dogs a lot or goes on family bike rides. She seems to prefer being outside in the sunshine rather than being cooped up inside on a treadmill or rowing machine.

Writing

Miley is passionate about writing. She loves to sit down with a notebook and pen and coming up with lyrics or write other things. She is very creative and writing is what she likes doing the most in her spare time. It allows her to express herself and let off steam.

Miley is writing a book called *The Diary of Priscilla's Coffeehouse* about some people she met at a coffee shop. Sadly for Miley fans she isn't planning on releasing it – she just wants to keep it for herself. Hopefully she might change her mind one day.

When Miley is writing pop songs she usually starts by making beats and then adds lyrics to that. Her ballads usually come together from notes she has made about how she's feeling. She doesn't set out to turn how she is feeling into songs but sometimes it just happens that way: she'll be writing and suddenly think, 'That would make a good song, and help people going through a similar situation.'

X is for...

X Factor

Miley loves performing on big TV shows and she was thrilled to get invited to perform on *The X Factor*. She had an interview with Holly Willoughby after her performance and was able to express how she feels about *X Factor*-style shows. She said: 'I think it's a really good opportunity because the hardest part is getting used to being on stage. If I watch from my very first [*Hannah Montana*] show, and I watch now, I'm a completely different performer. So I think when you do get a deal or you do start doing concerts you'll be a lot better because you've had so much practice so it just gives you free tries.'

She also had advice for the younger contestants. 'Every time they critique you, I think really take it in because you'll always get notes and you've got to learn how to take those, and you need to learn how to take them without getting upset first because I would always get upset when people would give me notes. And now it's really good that I'm able to take them because it makes me a better performer,' she said.

On Simon Cowell when he gives nasty comments, Miley said: 'I think always be respectful, because he's still your judge and he's only trying to help, but there will always be a "Simon" in your life, no matter what you do, no matter what kind of job you have. You always have someone like that. I think its good because… you can have the best voice of all history; there'll always be something you can improve on. And you should never be "I'm the best, I'm the best". You need someone like Simon to tell you that you're not the best. So there's other things that you need to do. And sometimes he takes it a little far, but I think that's good because then you know what you can handle. It'll be better for you as you'll grow stronger as a person.'

Miley didn't get to see the 2009 winner Joe McElderry perform his track 'The Climb' (which was his first single and Christmas number 2) live. She checked it out on YouTube and was impressed with his version, although she thinks it would be better if *The X Factor* winner got to win and then released a song a while after, like they do on *American Idol*. That way when they sing the song they can be concentrating on just that, not the fact that they have just won.

Y is for...

YouTube

In February 2008 Miley and her best friend Mandy decided to have some fun and make some videos of them hanging out and joking around. They posted the first one on YouTube under the title *The Miley and Mandy Show*. It was a big hit with fans and they set about filming more videos. The first four episodes of *The Miley and Mandy Show* were viewed by more than one million people (in total) in just a few weeks. It's thought that the girls decided to do the show because Miley got a new computer. They film the videos, pick the music and then Miley edits it all together into a great episode.

The majority of the episodes are filmed in Miley's bedroom, something fans love because it means they get to see more of Miley's world. Because Miley and Mandy have been really busy they haven't posted any new episodes on YouTube since September 2009. They will make more when they can but for now Miley is just posting her own videos.

In April 2010 Miley announced on her blog: 'Hey guys! I made my own youtube account so I can upload more videos for yall! I will continue to do videos for Mworld but for some reason it's not working on my computer right now! I'm gonna make my youtube account more for my older fans and then do constant updates for my younger fans on Mileyworld! My youtube account is Youtube/MCFORREALZZZ! I haven't uploaded any videos yet but I will soon! love you guys! Hope all is well!'

In June 2010 Miley posted a video of cool photos of the Cyrus family on holiday in Cabo San Lucas, Mexico. She likes sharing her life with her fans and only one month after posting it had been viewed nearly two million times.

Miley is very popular on YouTube and there are

thousands of videos of her auditions, interviews, performances and more for you to check out.

Z is for...

Zac Efron

Miley may have dated some gorgeous guys in the past, but she still fancies Zac Efron. She can't help but think he's super hot and she loved seeing him in the *High School Musical* movies. She admits that the reason she watches Zac Efron movies is because he's hot... and secondly, he's a good actor. She says he's got a special place in her heart.

In many ways this makes her just like any other teenage girl – but she can't put Zac Efron posters on her bedroom wall because he's her friend and it would freak him out. Zac revealed to *Access Hollywood*: 'I've known her since she was a little girl. It's amazing what she's done. She's blossomed into this beautiful lady and is taking the world by storm. I'm so proud of her.'

Zebra

When Miley was a child her grandad bought her a real live donkey for a present. She was so happy and named him Eeyore. Her grandad told her that Eeyore was half zebra because he had white ankles. He was only joking but Miley believed him. She didn't realise that all donkeys have white ankles!

Miley's living room has zebra-print armchairs. They are really funky. She seems to love zebras: her seventeenth birthday cake had two of its four layers covered in zebra-style icing.

Zits

Miley might look perfect on the cover of magazines but it isn't the real Miley we are seeing. She doesn't have perfect skin.

Her dad had bad skin when he was a teenager but in many ways it's harder for Miley because she's a girl and people keep making nasty comments about her skin on the internet. She has problems with zits like any other teenager but hers aren't helped by the fact she wears so much make-up when she's filming. Her pictures are often photo-shopped to give her perfect skin because as a celebrity she's supposed to have flawless skin.

She confessed to oceanUP: 'I think even though people always see me with makeup I still break out, even though everyone thinks I don't. And I hate it! I'm the worst at dealing with zits. And I get in such a bad mood when I break out and all I can think is that people are only looking at my skin!'

To try and combat her bad skin Miley always makes sure she washes her face thoroughly before she goes to bed. She doesn't go on sleepovers any more because she feels that she can't clean her face properly when she's not at home. She always uses organic products now and thinks it helps her skin. Miley must be dying for the day her teenage zits disappear because she'll never have to stress about her face again.